"After utilizing toolkits from The Art of Service, I was able to identify threats within my organization to which I was completely unaware. Using my team's knowledge as a competitive advantage, we now have superior systems that save time and energy."

"As a new Chief Technology Officer, I was feeling unprepared and inadequate to be successful in my role. I ordered an IT toolkit Sunday night and was prepared Monday morning to shed light on areas of improvement within my organization. I no longer felt overwhelmed and intimidated, I was excited to share what I had learned."

"I used the questionnaires to interview members of my team. I never knew how many insights we could produce collectively with our internal knowledge."

"I usually work until at least 8pm on weeknights. The Art of Service questionnaire saved me so much time and worry that Thursday night I attended my son's soccer game without sacrificing my professional obligations."

"After purchasing The Art of Service toolkit, I was able to identify areas where my company was not in compliance that could have put my job at risk. I looked like a hero when I proactively educated my team on the risks and presented a solid solution."

"I spent months shopping for an external consultant before realizing that The Art of Service would allow my team to consult themselves! Not only did we save time not catching a consultant up to speed, we were able to keep our company information and industry secrets confidential."

"Everyday there are new regulations and processes in my industry. The Art of Service toolkit has kept me ahead by using AI technology to constantly update the toolkits and address emerging needs."

"I customized The Art of Service toolkit to focus specifically on the concerns of my role and industry. I didn't have to waste time with a generic self-help book that wasn't tailored to my exact situation."

"Many of our competitors have asked us about our secret sauce. When I tell them it's the knowledge we have in-house, they never believe me. Little do they know The Art of Service toolkits are working behind the scenes."

"One of my friends hired a consultant who used the knowledge gained working with his company to advise their competitor. Talk about a competitive disadvantage! The Art of Service allowed us to keep our knowledge from walking out the door along with a huge portion of our budget in consulting fees."

"Honestly, I didn't know what I didn't know. Before purchasing The Art of Service, I didn't realize how many areas of my business needed to be refreshed and improved. I am so relieved The Art of Service was there to highlight our blind spots."

"Before The Art of Service, I waited eagerly for consulting company reports to come out each month. These reports kept us up to speed but provided little value because they put our competitors on the same playing field. With The Art of Service, we have uncovered unique insights to drive our business forward."

"Instead of investing extensive resources into an external consultant, we can spend more of our budget towards pursuing our company goals and objectives…while also spending a little more on corporate holiday parties."

"The risk of our competitors getting ahead has been mitigated because The Art of Service has provided us with a 360-degree view of threats within our organization before they even arise."

Enterprise Integration Patterns
Complete Self-Assessment Guide

Notice of rights

You are licensed to use the Self-Assessment contents in your presentations and materials for internal use and customers without asking us - we are here to help.

All rights reserved for the book itself: this book may not be reproduced or transmitted in any form by any means, electronic, mechanical, photocopying, recording, or otherwise, without the prior written permission of the publisher.

The information in this book is distributed on an "As Is" basis without warranty. While every precaution has been taken in the preparation of the book, neither the author nor the publisher shall have any liability to any person or entity with respect to any loss or damage caused or alleged to be caused directly or indirectly by the instructions contained in this book or by the products described in it.

Trademarks

Many of the designations used by manufacturers and sellers to distinguish their products are claimed as trademarks. Where those designations appear in this book, and the publisher was aware of a trademark claim, the designations appear as requested by the owner of the trademark. All other product names and services identified throughout this book are used in editorial fashion only and for the benefit of such companies with no intention of infringement of the trademark. No such use, or the use of any trade name, is intended to convey endorsement or other affiliation with this book.

Copyright © by The Art of Service
https://theartofservice.com
support@theartofservice.com

Table of Contents

About The Art of Service   10

Included Resources - how to access   10
Purpose of this Self-Assessment   12
How to use the Self-Assessment   13
Enterprise Integration Patterns
Scorecard Example   15
Enterprise Integration Patterns
Scorecard   16

BEGINNING OF THE
SELF-ASSESSMENT: 17
CRITERION #1: RECOGNIZE   18

CRITERION #2: DEFINE: 29

CRITERION #3: MEASURE: 41

CRITERION #4: ANALYZE: 49

CRITERION #5: IMPROVE: 65

CRITERION #6: CONTROL: 76

CRITERION #7: SUSTAIN: 85
Enterprise Integration Patterns and Managing Projects,
Criteria for Project Managers: 138
1.0 Initiating Process Group: Enterprise Integration Patterns
                                                                 139

1.1 Project Charter: Enterprise Integration Patterns   141

1.2 Stakeholder Register: Enterprise Integration Patterns 143

1.3 Stakeholder Analysis Matrix: Enterprise Integration
Patterns   144

2.0 Planning Process Group: Enterprise Integration Patterns 146

2.1 Project Management Plan: Enterprise Integration Patterns 148

2.2 Scope Management Plan: Enterprise Integration Patterns 150

2.3 Requirements Management Plan: Enterprise Integration Patterns 152

2.4 Requirements Documentation: Enterprise Integration Patterns 154

2.5 Requirements Traceability Matrix: Enterprise Integration Patterns 156

2.6 Project Scope Statement: Enterprise Integration Patterns 158

2.7 Assumption and Constraint Log: Enterprise Integration Patterns 160

2.8 Work Breakdown Structure: Enterprise Integration Patterns 162

2.9 WBS Dictionary: Enterprise Integration Patterns 164

2.10 Schedule Management Plan: Enterprise Integration Patterns 167

2.11 Activity List: Enterprise Integration Patterns 169

2.12 Activity Attributes: Enterprise Integration Patterns 171

2.13 Milestone List: Enterprise Integration Patterns 173

2.14 Network Diagram: Enterprise Integration Patterns   175

2.15 Activity Resource Requirements: Enterprise Integration Patterns   177

2.16 Resource Breakdown Structure: Enterprise Integration Patterns   178

2.17 Activity Duration Estimates: Enterprise Integration Patterns   180

2.18 Duration Estimating Worksheet: Enterprise Integration Patterns   183

2.19 Project Schedule: Enterprise Integration Patterns   185

2.20 Cost Management Plan: Enterprise Integration Patterns   187

2.21 Activity Cost Estimates: Enterprise Integration Patterns   189

2.22 Cost Estimating Worksheet: Enterprise Integration Patterns   191

2.23 Cost Baseline: Enterprise Integration Patterns   193

2.24 Quality Management Plan: Enterprise Integration Patterns   195

2.25 Quality Metrics: Enterprise Integration Patterns   197

2.26 Process Improvement Plan: Enterprise Integration Patterns   199

2.27 Responsibility Assignment Matrix: Enterprise Integration Patterns   201

2.28 Roles and Responsibilities: Enterprise Integration Patterns   203

2.29 Human Resource Management Plan: Enterprise Integration Patterns   205

2.30 Communications Management Plan: Enterprise Integration Patterns   207

2.31 Risk Management Plan: Enterprise Integration Patterns   209

2.32 Risk Register: Enterprise Integration Patterns   211

2.33 Probability and Impact Assessment: Enterprise Integration Patterns   213

2.34 Probability and Impact Matrix: Enterprise Integration Patterns   215

2.35 Risk Data Sheet: Enterprise Integration Patterns   217

2.36 Procurement Management Plan: Enterprise Integration Patterns   219

2.37 Source Selection Criteria: Enterprise Integration Patterns   221

2.38 Stakeholder Management Plan: Enterprise Integration Patterns   223

2.39 Change Management Plan: Enterprise Integration Patterns   225

3.0 Executing Process Group: Enterprise Integration Patterns   227

3.1 Team Member Status Report: Enterprise Integration Patterns 229

3.2 Change Request: Enterprise Integration Patterns 231

3.3 Change Log: Enterprise Integration Patterns 233

3.4 Decision Log: Enterprise Integration Patterns 235

3.5 Quality Audit: Enterprise Integration Patterns 237

3.6 Team Directory: Enterprise Integration Patterns 240

3.7 Team Operating Agreement: Enterprise Integration Patterns 242

3.8 Team Performance Assessment: Enterprise Integration Patterns 244

3.9 Team Member Performance Assessment: Enterprise Integration Patterns 246

3.10 Issue Log: Enterprise Integration Patterns 248

4.0 Monitoring and Controlling Process Group: Enterprise Integration Patterns 250

4.1 Project Performance Report: Enterprise Integration Patterns 252

4.2 Variance Analysis: Enterprise Integration Patterns 254

4.3 Earned Value Status: Enterprise Integration Patterns 256

4.4 Risk Audit: Enterprise Integration Patterns 258

4.5 Contractor Status Report: Enterprise Integration Patterns 260

4.6 Formal Acceptance: Enterprise Integration Patterns   262

5.0 Closing Process Group: Enterprise Integration Patterns
                                                          264

5.1 Procurement Audit: Enterprise Integration Patterns   266

5.2 Contract Close-Out: Enterprise Integration Patterns   268

5.3 Project or Phase Close-Out: Enterprise Integration
Patterns   270

5.4 Lessons Learned: Enterprise Integration Patterns   272
Index   274

About The Art of Service

The Art of Service, Business Process Architects since 2000, is dedicated to helping stakeholders achieve excellence.

Defining, designing, creating, and implementing a process to solve a stakeholders challenge or meet an objective is the most valuable role… In EVERY group, company, organization and department.

Unless you're talking a one-time, single-use project, there should be a process. Whether that process is managed and implemented by humans, AI, or a combination of the two, it needs to be designed by someone with a complex enough perspective to ask the right questions.

Someone capable of asking the right questions and step back and say, 'What are we really trying to accomplish here? And is there a different way to look at it?'

With The Art of Service's Self-Assessments, we empower people who can do just that — whether their title is marketer, entrepreneur, manager, salesperson, consultant, Business Process Manager, executive assistant, IT Manager, CIO etc... —they are the people who rule the future. They are people who watch the process as it happens, and ask the right questions to make the process work better.

Contact us when you need any support with this Self-Assessment and any help with templates, blue-prints and examples of standard documents you might need:

https://theartofservice.com
support@theartofservice.com

Included Resources - how to access

Included with your purchase of the book is the Enterprise

Integration Patterns Self-Assessment Spreadsheet Dashboard which contains all questions and Self-Assessment areas and auto-generates insights, graphs, and project RACI planning - all with examples to get you started right away.

How? Simply send an email to
access@theartofservice.com
with this books' title in the subject to get the Enterprise Integration Patterns Self Assessment Tool right away.

The auto reply will guide you further, you will then receive the following contents with New and Updated specific criteria:

- The latest quick edition of the book in PDF

- The latest complete edition of the book in PDF, which criteria correspond to the criteria in...

- The Self-Assessment Excel Dashboard, and...

- Example pre-filled Self-Assessment Excel Dashboard to get familiar with results generation

- In-depth specific Checklists covering the topic

- Project management checklists and templates to assist with implementation

INCLUDES LIFETIME SELF ASSESSMENT UPDATES

Every self assessment comes with Lifetime Updates and Lifetime Free Updated Books. Lifetime Updates is an industry-first feature which allows you to receive verified self assessment updates, ensuring you always have the most accurate information at your fingertips.

Get it now- you will be glad you did - do it now, before you forget.

Send an email to **access@theartofservice.com** with this books' title in the subject to get the Enterprise Integration Patterns Self Assessment Tool right away.

Purpose of this Self-Assessment

This Self-Assessment has been developed to improve understanding of the requirements and elements of Enterprise Integration Patterns, based on best practices and standards in business process architecture, design and quality management.

It is designed to allow for a rapid Self-Assessment to determine how closely existing management practices and procedures correspond to the elements of the Self-Assessment.

The criteria of requirements and elements of Enterprise Integration Patterns have been rephrased in the format of a Self-Assessment questionnaire, with a seven-criterion scoring system, as explained in this document.

In this format, even with limited background knowledge of Enterprise Integration Patterns, a manager can quickly review existing operations to determine how they measure up to the standards. This in turn can serve as the starting point of a 'gap analysis' to identify management tools or system elements that might usefully be implemented in the organization to help improve overall performance.

How to use the Self-Assessment

On the following pages are a series of questions to identify to what extent your Enterprise Integration Patterns initiative is complete in comparison to the requirements set in standards.

To facilitate answering the questions, there is a space in front of each question to enter a score on a scale of '1' to '5'.

    1 Strongly Disagree

    2 Disagree

    3 Neutral

    4 Agree

    5 Strongly Agree

Read the question and rate it with the following in front of mind:

'In my belief, the answer to this question is clearly defined'.

There are two ways in which you can choose to interpret this statement;
1. how aware are you that the answer to the question is clearly defined
2. for more in-depth analysis you can choose to gather evidence and confirm the answer to the question. This obviously will take more time, most Self-Assessment users opt for the first way to interpret the question and dig deeper later on based on the outcome of the overall Self-Assessment.

A score of '1' would mean that the answer is not clear at all, where a '5' would mean the answer is crystal clear and defined. Leave emtpy when the question is not applicable or you don't want to answer it, you can skip it without affecting your score. Write your score in the space provided.

After you have responded to all the appropriate statements in each section, compute your average score for that section, using the formula provided, and round to the nearest tenth. Then transfer to the corresponding spoke in the Enterprise Integration Patterns Scorecard on the second next page of the Self-Assessment.

Your completed Enterprise Integration Patterns Scorecard will give you a clear presentation of which Enterprise Integration Patterns areas need attention.

Enterprise Integration Patterns Scorecard Example

Example of how the finalized Scorecard can look like:

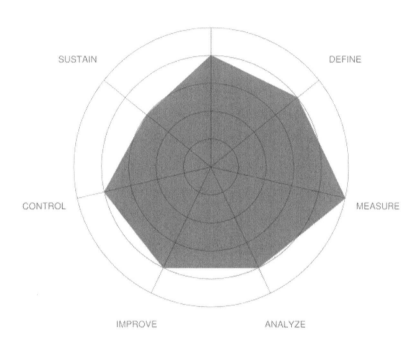

Enterprise Integration Patterns Scorecard

Your Scores:

BEGINNING OF THE SELF-ASSESSMENT:

CRITERION #1: RECOGNIZE

INTENT: Be aware of the need for change. Recognize that there is an unfavorable variation, problem or symptom.

In my belief, the answer to this question is clearly defined:

5 Strongly Agree

4 Agree

3 Neutral

2 Disagree

1 Strongly Disagree

1. How will you recognize and celebrate results?
<--- Score

2. What are some key issues related to IT project staffing that need to be well managed?
<--- Score

3. When a Enterprise Integration Patterns manager recognizes a problem, what options are available?

<--- Score

4. When and how do you application need updates from other applications?
<--- Score

5. Does Enterprise Integration Patterns create potential expectations in other areas that need to be recognized and considered?
<--- Score

6. What is the recognized need?
<--- Score

7. What is event based integration?
<--- Score

8. How often would you need to run the integration?
<--- Score

9. How widespread are the needs for application integration?
<--- Score

10. How will the application be supported in the event of errors or outages?
<--- Score

11. To what extent does management recognize Enterprise Integration Patterns as a tool to increase the results?
<--- Score

12. What type of applications are needed?
<--- Score

13. How are the Enterprise Integration Patterns's objectives aligned to the group's overall stakeholder strategy?
<--- Score

14. How do you recognize an Enterprise Integration Patterns objection?
<--- Score

15. To what extent does each concerned units management team recognize Enterprise Integration Patterns as an effective investment?
<--- Score

16. What business problems does soa address?
<--- Score

17. What are your business needs, and what should the integration allow you to do?
<--- Score

18. Can management personnel recognize the monetary benefit of Enterprise Integration Patterns?
<--- Score

19. How much are sponsors, customers, partners, stakeholders involved in Enterprise Integration Patterns? In other words, what are the risks, if Enterprise Integration Patterns does not deliver successfully?
<--- Score

20. What does the IT organization need?
<--- Score

21. What type of applications do users need to be more productive?
<--- Score

22. Will you need to plug in more applications in the future?
<--- Score

23. What are their key business issues?
<--- Score

24. To what extent would your organization benefit from being recognized as a award recipient?
<--- Score

25. Are controls defined to recognize and contain problems?
<--- Score

26. What would happen if Enterprise Integration Patterns weren't done?
<--- Score

27. What situation(s) led to this Enterprise Integration Patterns Self Assessment?
<--- Score

28. What non procurement applications will need to be integrated with any new procurement applications?
<--- Score

29. Who else hopes to benefit from it?
<--- Score

30. What would you have done in retrospect to have prevented that problem from happening?
<--- Score

31. Is there any software that needs to be loaded onto local computers?
<--- Score

32. What are the most appropriate ways in which integration problems need to be solved?
<--- Score

33. How are you going to measure success?
<--- Score

34. What do you need to make messaging work?
<--- Score

35. What are the core services needed to optimize the business?
<--- Score

36. Which business units need to be involved in the project?
<--- Score

37. Would you recognize a threat from the inside?
<--- Score

38. Do you recognize Enterprise Integration Patterns achievements?
<--- Score

39. Will a response program recognize when a crisis occurs and provide some level of response?

<--- Score

40. Are there any specific expectations or concerns about the Enterprise Integration Patterns team, Enterprise Integration Patterns itself?
<--- Score

41. How do you distinguish good software requirements from problematic ones?
<--- Score

42. What does Enterprise Integration Patterns success mean to the stakeholders?
<--- Score

43. Are losses recognized in a timely manner?
<--- Score

44. How to satisfy the needs of all the users of the enterprise fast?
<--- Score

45. Are employees recognized for desired behaviors?
<--- Score

46. Do you need to deploy a single component to several nodes to support failover within your system?
<--- Score

47. What are the expected benefits of Enterprise Integration Patterns to the stakeholder?
<--- Score

48. Are employees recognized or rewarded for

performance that demonstrates the highest levels of integrity?

<--- Score

49. What integration capabilities do you need?

<--- Score

50. What do you need to integrate mobile devices throughout your enterprise?

<--- Score

51. What enterprise and/or business application training do your employees, customers, or other users need?

<--- Score

52. What is preventing further enhancement of the capabilities?

<--- Score

53. Do you need the interface to be supported by SAP?

<--- Score

54. What are the stakeholder objectives to be achieved with Enterprise Integration Patterns?

<--- Score

55. Do you need different information or graphics?

<--- Score

56. Which interfaces do you need to implement?

<--- Score

57. What is your Enterprise Architecture strategy to help IT support your business needs?

<--- Score

58. As a sponsor, customer or management, how important is it to meet goals, objectives?
<--- Score

59. Are you unsure whether your organization even needs to integrate its enterprise wide systems?
<--- Score

60. What integration, if any, needs to occur with back end IT systems?
<--- Score

61. What pitfalls does your organization need to avoid in integration projects?
<--- Score

62. Are there recognized Enterprise Integration Patterns problems?
<--- Score

63. What are the minority interests and what amount of minority interests can be recognized?
<--- Score

64. Will one or more of their key issues be resolved by the project?
<--- Score

65. How do you recognize an objection?
<--- Score

66. How long does the system need to run without failure?

<--- Score

67. How could it do preventative or predictive maintenance?
<--- Score

68. Will new tools, applications, and IT infrastructure be needed?
<--- Score

69. Does the application have maintenance issues that affect business operations?
<--- Score

70. Are Enterprise Integration Patterns changes recognized early enough to be approved through the regular process?
<--- Score

71. What system tests need to be run?
<--- Score

72. What practices helps your organization to develop its capacity to recognize patterns?
<--- Score

73. Is the need for organizational change recognized?
<--- Score

74. What other technology factors may be problematic when implementing an integration project?
<--- Score

75. Should you invest in industry-recognized

qualifications?
<--- Score

76. What does the application need to do with it?
<--- Score

77. Do any of their needs conflict with other stakeholders?
<--- Score

78. Are their needs included or involved in the project?
<--- Score

79. What is agile integration and why is it needed?
<--- Score

80. What problems are you facing and how do you consider Enterprise Integration Patterns will circumvent those obstacles?
<--- Score

81. How do you stay flexible and focused to recognize larger Enterprise Integration Patterns results?
<--- Score

82. What types of skills have been identified as important for successful IT project managers?
<--- Score

Add up total points for this section:
_____ = Total points for this section

Divided by: _____ (number of statements answered) = _____

Average score for this section

Transfer your score to the Enterprise Integration Patterns Index at the beginning of the Self-Assessment.

CRITERION #2: DEFINE:

INTENT: Formulate the stakeholder problem. Define the problem, needs and objectives.

In my belief, the answer to this question is clearly defined:

5 Strongly Agree

4 Agree

3 Neutral

2 Disagree

1 Strongly Disagree

1. What specific workflow applications are required to be included in the scope of services, if any?
<--- Score

2. Should a defined service operation be synchronous or asynchronous?
<--- Score

3. Is the team formed and are team leaders (Coaches and Management Leads) assigned?
<--- Score

4. Is the Enterprise Integration Patterns scope manageable?
<--- Score

5. How do enterprises meet the requirements to make best use of collaboration?
<--- Score

6. How will variation in the actual durations of each activity be dealt with to ensure that the expected Enterprise Integration Patterns results are met?
<--- Score

7. What specifically is the problem? Where does it occur? When does it occur? What is its extent?
<--- Score

8. Is the other bounded context a legacy system?
<--- Score

9. Which industrial and mobile applications require multimedia application integration?
<--- Score

10. Are different versions of process maps needed to account for the different types of inputs?
<--- Score

11. Who are the Enterprise Integration Patterns improvement team members, including Management Leads and Coaches?
<--- Score

12. How does the employer organize the work and define the available positions?
<--- Score

13. Are stakeholder processes mapped?
<--- Score

14. Do you have stand alone applications testing requirement?
<--- Score

15. Is there a critical path to deliver Enterprise Integration Patterns results?
<--- Score

16. How is the team tracking and documenting its work?
<--- Score

17. When are meeting minutes sent out? Who is on the distribution list?
<--- Score

18. When is/was the Enterprise Integration Patterns start date?
<--- Score

19. Has/have the customer(s) been identified?
<--- Score

20. What are the compelling stakeholder reasons for embarking on Enterprise Integration Patterns?
<--- Score

21. Which is a main business requirement in the

financial services industry?
<--- Score

22. Are there different segments of customers?
<--- Score

23. Is the application flexible and able to meet changing business requirements?
<--- Score

24. Is a fully trained team formed, supported, and committed to work on the Enterprise Integration Patterns improvements?
<--- Score

25. Is data collected and displayed to better understand customer(s) critical needs and requirements.
<--- Score

26. Is Enterprise Integration Patterns linked to key stakeholder goals and objectives?
<--- Score

27. How did the Enterprise Integration Patterns manager receive input to the development of a Enterprise Integration Patterns improvement plan and the estimated completion dates/times of each activity?
<--- Score

28. What is the network overhead of calling directly into the other bounded context?
<--- Score

29. Does the code work only for upper case letters?

<--- Score

30. Has a high-level 'as is' process map been completed, verified and validated?
<--- Score

31. Where is the boundary between information gathering and the violation of personal integrity?
<--- Score

32. Does the product require an Application Server?
<--- Score

33. Is the team adequately staffed with the desired cross-functionality? If not, what additional resources are available to the team?
<--- Score

34. Will team members regularly document their Enterprise Integration Patterns work?
<--- Score

35. How many hours of on site work will be required?
<--- Score

36. What are the particular requirements for cloud integration?
<--- Score

37. What is the number of systems / applications in scope for the engagement?
<--- Score

38. Are team charters developed?

<--- Score

39. How was the 'as is' process map developed, reviewed, verified and validated?
<--- Score

40. If substitutes have been appointed, have they been briefed on the Enterprise Integration Patterns goals and received regular communications as to the progress to date?
<--- Score

41. How will the Enterprise Integration Patterns team and the group measure complete success of Enterprise Integration Patterns?
<--- Score

42. What are the rough order estimates on cost savings/opportunities that Enterprise Integration Patterns brings?
<--- Score

43. Has a project plan, Gantt chart, or similar been developed/completed?
<--- Score

44. Are customers identified and high impact areas defined?
<--- Score

45. What are the Roles and Responsibilities for each team member and its leadership? Where is this documented?
<--- Score

46. Is Enterprise Integration Patterns currently on

schedule according to the plan?
<--- Score

47. What are the dynamics of the communication plan?
<--- Score

48. When is the estimated completion date?
<--- Score

49. Is the current 'as is' process being followed? If not, what are the discrepancies?
<--- Score

50. Has a team charter been developed and communicated?
<--- Score

51. Are there any constraints known that bear on the ability to perform Enterprise Integration Patterns work? How is the team addressing them?
<--- Score

52. Will your new application require integration with incumbent software systems?
<--- Score

53. Is the improvement team aware of the different versions of a process: what they think it is vs. what it actually is vs. what it should be vs. what it could be?
<--- Score

54. Is there regularly 100% attendance at the team meetings? If not, have appointed substitutes attended to preserve cross-functionality and full representation?

<--- Score

55. What kind of enterprise integration is required?

<--- Score

56. Is the application capable of sensor integration as compass, gyroscope or accelerometer?

<--- Score

57. Is scanner integration required?

<--- Score

58. Will team members perform Enterprise Integration Patterns work when assigned and in a timely fashion?

<--- Score

59. What critical content must be communicated – who, what, when, where, and how?

<--- Score

60. Does it require efficient enterprise application integration?

<--- Score

61. How often are the team meetings?

<--- Score

62. What key stakeholder process output measure(s) does Enterprise Integration Patterns leverage and how?

<--- Score

63. Has the improvement team collected the 'voice of the customer' (obtained feedback – qualitative and quantitative)?

<--- Score

64. Does your organization have any unique requirements relating to enterprise business applications?
<--- Score

65. Has anyone else (internal or external to the group) attempted to solve this problem or a similar one before? If so, what knowledge can be leveraged from these previous efforts?
<--- Score

66. What customer feedback methods were used to solicit their input?
<--- Score

67. Has everyone on the team, including the team leaders, been properly trained?
<--- Score

68. Has the direction changed at all during the course of Enterprise Integration Patterns? If so, when did it change and why?
<--- Score

69. Are there cases where integration to more than one application or repository is required?
<--- Score

70. Is there a completed, verified, and validated high-level 'as is' (not 'should be' or 'could be') stakeholder process map?
<--- Score

71. Have the customer needs been translated into

specific, measurable requirements? How?
<--- Score

72. Are improvement team members fully trained on Enterprise Integration Patterns?
<--- Score

73. Is there a completed SIPOC representation, describing the Suppliers, Inputs, Process, Outputs, and Customers?
<--- Score

74. What are the boundaries of the scope? What is in bounds and what is not? What is the start point? What is the stop point?
<--- Score

75. Is the team equipped with available and reliable resources?
<--- Score

76. Which general strategy, your organization must adopt, to fulfill its mobile integration requirements?
<--- Score

77. What constraints exist that might impact the team?
<--- Score

78. Do the problem and goal statements meet the SMART criteria (specific, measurable, attainable, relevant, and time-bound)?
<--- Score

79. Does the team have regular meetings?

<--- Score

80. What security protocols does that application require?
<--- Score

81. How does the Enterprise Integration Patterns manager ensure against scope creep?
<--- Score

82. Has the Enterprise Integration Patterns work been fairly and/or equitably divided and delegated among team members who are qualified and capable to perform the work? Has everyone contributed?
<--- Score

83. What would be the goal or target for a Enterprise Integration Patterns's improvement team?
<--- Score

84. Is there a Enterprise Integration Patterns management charter, including stakeholder case, problem and goal statements, scope, milestones, roles and responsibilities, communication plan?
<--- Score

85. Is the team sponsored by a champion or stakeholder leader?
<--- Score

86. Are customer(s) identified and segmented according to their different needs and requirements?
<--- Score

87. How do you keep key subject matter experts in the loop?

<--- Score

88. How to gather usage statistics on channel level?
<--- Score

89. Is full participation by members in regularly held team meetings guaranteed?
<--- Score

Add up total points for this section:
_____ = Total points for this section

Divided by: _____ (number of statements answered) = _____
Average score for this section

Transfer your score to the Enterprise Integration Patterns Index at the beginning of the Self-Assessment.

CRITERION #3: MEASURE:

INTENT: Gather the correct data. Measure the current performance and evolution of the situation.

In my belief, the answer to this question is clearly defined:

5 Strongly Agree

4 Agree

3 Neutral

2 Disagree

1 Strongly Disagree

1. Are high impact defects defined and identified in the stakeholder process?
<--- Score

2. What is the impact on other IT systems?
<--- Score

3. What are the agreed upon definitions of the high impact areas, defect(s), unit(s), and opportunities that

will figure into the process capability metrics?
<--- Score

4. What are the projected cost/benefit savings for migration?
<--- Score

5. Does the projects success create any negative impact for the stakeholder?
<--- Score

6. How to measure the usage of content within integration scenarios?
<--- Score

7. Are the application maintenance costs reducing?
<--- Score

8. How many people in their organization are directly impacted by the project?
<--- Score

9. How to measure usage statistics and behavior of a component?
<--- Score

10. What project goals can be eliminate or revised to remove the negative impact?
<--- Score

11. What data was collected (past, present, future/ongoing)?
<--- Score

12. Who participated in the data collection for

measurements?
<--- Score

13. How do you build services that are scalable in a simple and cost effective way?
<--- Score

14. How is a single measurement value generated?
<--- Score

15. Are key measures identified and agreed upon?
<--- Score

16. How should applications integration be measured?
<--- Score

17. Is data collected on key measures that were identified?
<--- Score

18. Does data ownership cause a problem?
<--- Score

19. What charts has the team used to display the components of variation in the process?
<--- Score

20. What are the key input variables? What are the key process variables? What are the key output variables?
<--- Score

21. Is data collection planned and executed?
<--- Score

22. What are your critical business priorities and

strategies?
<--- Score

23. What priorities do you share with other stakeholders?
<--- Score

24. Is Process Variation Displayed/Communicated?
<--- Score

25. Will the cost of hosted services balance out against any existing licensing arrangements or Enterprise Agreement?
<--- Score

26. How can tactical projects impact the buildout of the services catalog?
<--- Score

27. What key measures identified indicate the performance of the stakeholder process?
<--- Score

28. Can the system be implemented in a cost effective manner?
<--- Score

29. How large is the gap between current performance and the customer-specified (goal) performance?
<--- Score

30. How much are the current application maintenance costs?
<--- Score

31. Does installation require high integration costs?
<--- Score

32. How do you effectively analyze and debug the flow of messages in a loosely coupled system?
<--- Score

33. What has the team done to assure the stability and accuracy of the measurement process?
<--- Score

34. Which methods cause problem in your work?
<--- Score

35. Is key measure data collection planned and executed, process variation displayed and communicated and performance baselined?
<--- Score

36. What is the impact of excluding stakeholders needs?
<--- Score

37. Is long term and short term variability accounted for?
<--- Score

38. How much of a priority are digital initiatives for your organization?
<--- Score

39. How close to budget were the final project costs?
<--- Score

40. Do you use IT to increase your customers costs of switching to a new supplier?
<--- Score

41. What particular quality tools did the team find helpful in establishing measurements?
<--- Score

42. How are analytical results integrated with business processes, as applications and workflows?
<--- Score

43. Have you found any 'ground fruit' or 'low-hanging fruit' for immediate remedies to the gap in performance?
<--- Score

44. What knowledge is provided by big data analytics?
<--- Score

45. What are the costs involved in implementation of integrated enterprise application platforms?
<--- Score

46. Are process variation components displayed/ communicated using suitable charts, graphs, plots?
<--- Score

47. Who is directly impacted by the project?
<--- Score

48. Will business analysts wire together components in visual tools?
<--- Score

49. Have you given thought to the impact to your organization of moving its production data store?
<--- Score

50. How is scalability and cost effectiveness in data integration achieved?
<--- Score

51. How exactly do you prioritize the migration of applications to the cloud?
<--- Score

52. Is a solid data collection plan established that includes measurement systems analysis?
<--- Score

53. Was a data collection plan established?
<--- Score

54. What kind of impact do the increased customer service demands have on present day logistics?
<--- Score

55. Is there a Performance Baseline?
<--- Score

56. How fast and at what cost do you change an application?
<--- Score

57. How much does it cost to maintain the current systems?
<--- Score

Add up total points for this section:

_____ = Total points for this section

Divided by: _____ (number of statements answered) = _____
Average score for this section

Transfer your score to the Enterprise Integration Patterns Index at the beginning of the Self-Assessment.

CRITERION #4: ANALYZE:

INTENT: Analyze causes, assumptions and hypotheses.

In my belief, the answer to this question is clearly defined:

5 Strongly Agree

4 Agree

3 Neutral

2 Disagree

1 Strongly Disagree

1. How difficult is it to determine what data are stored about the part of the business you manage?
<--- Score

2. How does your organization win acceptance for collaborative processes among distributors, vendors and customers?
<--- Score

3. What is your organization process?

<--- Score

4. What are the most important requirements that integration solutions must meet for B2B processes?
<--- Score

5. Did your enterprise re engineer any processes at the same time?
<--- Score

6. How does master data management assist in the management of multiple databases?
<--- Score

7. How can a process without a messaging client participate in messaging?
<--- Score

8. What are the basic functions of managing the data resource?
<--- Score

9. Do you need to retain the data for any reason?
<--- Score

10. How to inform about an important event during message processing?
<--- Score

11. What data formats does your enterprise rely on the most?
<--- Score

**12. How do you process messages that are semantically equivalent, and arrive in a different

format?
<--- Score

13. What is your data breach policy?
<--- Score

14. Is it machine generated or sentiment data?
<--- Score

15. How do systems using different data formats communicate with each other using messaging?
<--- Score

16. Do you need real time access to the latest data?
<--- Score

17. What is the purpose of business process modeling?
<--- Score

18. How do you minimize dependencies when integrating applications that use different data formats?
<--- Score

19. How can data accuracy, completeness, and timeliness be assured?
<--- Score

20. How are corporations handling metadata within their enterprise?
<--- Score

**21. How do you ensure information in enterprise applications is supporting agile operations, streamlined processes, and outstanding customer service?

<--- Score

22. What is a data dictionary and why is it important?

<--- Score

23. How do you increase a services adaptability to changing business processes?

<--- Score

24. How much computation is expected to be performed with data in memory?

<--- Score

25. How should ea be integrated with the budgeting process?

<--- Score

26. Where are the data center and storage facilities?

<--- Score

27. Who would be the master of the data?

<--- Score

28. What about database centric enterprise application integration?

<--- Score

29. How is the print process enacted?

<--- Score

30. Do you facilitate the smooth integration of your B2B infrastructure with your existing B2B solutions, enterprise applications, and business

processes?
<--- Score

31. How do you integrate your enterprise and cloud applications to your data warehouse in cloud?
<--- Score

32. Do you quickly integrate mobile applications with backend enterprise applications using minimal code?
<--- Score

33. Which vendors should you work with on Azure to build a complete cloud data management strategy?
<--- Score

34. Is the enterprise data topology centralized or decentralized?
<--- Score

35. Who executes activities in the immediate business process affected by the project?
<--- Score

36. How can the process oriented multimedia integration processing be realized and improved?
<--- Score

37. How to measure the usage of components during message processing?
<--- Score

38. Which data sources does your organization work with?

<--- Score

39. How to convert one data format to another?
<--- Score

40. How do you effectively use multiple processors?
<--- Score

41. How does a data warehouse differ from operational files or databases?
<--- Score

42. How to create reports when data is scattered within multiple services?
<--- Score

43. How is your organization approval process related to a cloud computing environment?
<--- Score

44. How will the project change their business processes?
<--- Score

45. Are there any additional business processes required to achieve the new services?
<--- Score

46. How do you perform complex processing on a message while maintaining independence and flexibility?
<--- Score

47. Are enterprise application solutions identified and recommended to support business processes?

<--- Score

48. How is the parse process enacted?
<--- Score

49. How are business processes orchestrated with application services in your organization?
<--- Score

50. How does your big data roadmap differ from one organized for any other emerging technology?
<--- Score

51. How do you choose a key for the data?
<--- Score

52. Is it possible to automate the entire software process?
<--- Score

53. How do you transmit a data item that the receiver will know how to process it?
<--- Score

54. How do you know where to send the data?
<--- Score

55. Are the business process services close to the enterprise business data?
<--- Score

56. How can multiple consumers on a single channel coordinate their message processing?
<--- Score

57. How much minimum time does it take to complete one process instance?
<--- Score

58. Have you adequately identified the skill sets necessary for evaluating big data technology?
<--- Score

59. What happens if the order cannot be processed by any system?
<--- Score

60. How is the transformation process enacted?
<--- Score

61. Do your key stakeholders believe that all the data has been moved?
<--- Score

62. How can systems using different data formats work together in the same architecture?
<--- Score

63. Should all applications and data be integrated?
<--- Score

64. What steps are you taking to share/socialize data within your organization?
<--- Score

65. What are some likely source data systems?
<--- Score

66. How can messages be sent confidential and with data privacy?
<--- Score

67. Is transaction processing required?
<--- Score

68. Should customer sales data be collected at point of sale or entered later?
<--- Score

69. How stable is the business process that will be executed in the service oriented system?
<--- Score

70. Have you considered your data needs for production?
<--- Score

71. How can systems using different data formats communicate with each other using messaging?
<--- Score

72. How can a messages data format be designed to allow for possible future changes?
<--- Score

73. What technologies will enable the multienterprise business process platform?
<--- Score

74. How to cancel the processing of a message?
<--- Score

75. How do you transfer packets of data?
<--- Score

76. What are the advantages of integrating labeling to enterprise applications and key sources

of label data?

<--- Score

77. Why should your organization choose to use an integrated database to store its operational data?

<--- Score

78. How do you repeat processing a message in a loop?

<--- Score

79. What happens if the originator process crashes after sending only a portion of the messages?

<--- Score

80. How do you route a message consecutively through a series of processing steps?

<--- Score

81. How quickly does your business identify and respond to change?

<--- Score

82. What are you getting from the data?

<--- Score

83. Why do other organizations often have several databases?

<--- Score

84. Is there a need to re engineer business processes or extend an existing business process?

<--- Score

85. Is the data formatted correctly?

<--- Score

86. How does aggregated reporting differ from direct access to each services internal database?
<--- Score

87. What happens if a request is processed twice?
<--- Score

88. What is business process execution?
<--- Score

89. What is the value of making better, more timely decisions with data sharing?
<--- Score

90. How do you pass only a subset of data to the request channel?
<--- Score

91. What data needs to be integrated on a regular basis?
<--- Score

92. Who are the people in your organization with experience, knowledge, or training in big data?
<--- Score

93. How often do services and their clients interact to exchange data?
<--- Score

94. Can the esb orchestrate back end business processes, including human workflow?
<--- Score

**95. How quickly do you resolve integration

breaks?

<--- Score

96. Is there a need for real time access to data?

<--- Score

97. How to execute custom code during message processing?

<--- Score

98. How is data linked or integrated into existing enterprise databases?

<--- Score

99. What happens to business resiliency when a problem occurs with the server, application, or data?

<--- Score

100. How do you get your data to Azure?

<--- Score

101. How can messaging be used to transfer data between applications?

<--- Score

102. Where does the enterprise business data reside?

<--- Score

103. Does the data support primary business processes?

<--- Score

104. What kind of business process is being automated?

<--- Score

105. Why do you need a software process?
<--- Score

106. Is the goal to make a process more efficient or to develop new products/services?
<--- Score

107. Why would you want to remove valuable data elements from a message?
<--- Score

108. How much time does your organization spend reconciling inconsistent data?
<--- Score

109. How many bottleneck areas do you see in the current process?
<--- Score

110. How can a messaging client process multiple messages concurrently?
<--- Score

111. Do you need to access small amounts of remote system data at any one time?
<--- Score

112. How do you separate the session data?
<--- Score

113. How will you validate that all your data has been moved?
<--- Score

114. How do you know what data format to use?
<--- Score

115. Are there increased risks to the security of sensitive data or your organization network?
<--- Score

116. What is the splitter delivering to the processing chain?
<--- Score

117. How are the applications, processes, and so on, aligned with the business strategies and goals?
<--- Score

118. Do you need to propagate context information between the successive steps of a process?
<--- Score

119. Is your data management platform well integrated into Azure?
<--- Score

120. What involvement is required from your organizations IT department to set up your integration processes?
<--- Score

121. Do you really want to discard data elements for good?
<--- Score

122. How valuable is business process integration to a firm?
<--- Score

123. How much maximum time does it take to complete one process instance?
<--- Score

124. What are the desired outcomes of the process?
<--- Score

125. Why adopt an existing software process, or improve your existing process using new techniques?
<--- Score

126. How could your organization add new reports quickly?
<--- Score

127. Why is a software process important?
<--- Score

128. What data must be stored in the system?
<--- Score

129. Who is responsible for data integration and strategy?
<--- Score

130. How can the application send a data item that the receiver will know how to process it?
<--- Score

131. What is the service of data enrichment?
<--- Score

**132. How should process activities and underlying

services communicate?
<--- Score

133. How will you do content management to refresh data?
<--- Score

134. How long does it take to execute one process execution?
<--- Score

135. How can messaging transmit an arbitrarily large amount of data?
<--- Score

136. Should the data be refreshed on a scheduled basis?
<--- Score

137. What happens to uses personal applications and data?
<--- Score

Add up total points for this section:
_____ = Total points for this section

Divided by: _____ (number of statements answered) = _____
Average score for this section

Transfer your score to the Enterprise Integration Patterns Index at the beginning of the Self-Assessment.

CRITERION #5: IMPROVE:

INTENT: Develop a practical solution. Innovate, establish and test the solution and to measure the results.

In my belief, the answer to this question is clearly defined:

5 Strongly Agree

4 Agree

3 Neutral

2 Disagree

1 Strongly Disagree

1. How do you combine the received messages into a single result message?
<--- Score

2. Are possible solutions generated and tested?
<--- Score

3. Are there any constraints (technical, political, cultural, or otherwise) that would inhibit certain

solutions?
<--- Score

4. Do you customize and extend a cloud based ERP solution to your business?
<--- Score

5. What lessons, if any, from a pilot were incorporated into the design of the full-scale solution?
<--- Score

6. Does the application allow performing of changes on business rules and decisions easily?
<--- Score

7. How many workflows need to be developed?
<--- Score

8. Are the best solutions selected?
<--- Score

9. How should developers approach new application development?
<--- Score

10. Is custom development and extensibility supported?
<--- Score

11. Which application area developed first?
<--- Score

12. Are new and improved process ('should be') maps developed?
<--- Score

13. How do enterprises manage the big digital transformation risks?
<--- Score

14. Does the solution use vendor approved integration points?
<--- Score

15. How can the executive board of your organization evaluate the benefit of an integration project?
<--- Score

16. Why is development of enterprise integration systems important?
<--- Score

17. How good is the information that people use to make their decisions?
<--- Score

18. How do you prepare the next generation of technology developers, administrators, and users so that security principles are more fully integrated?
<--- Score

19. How did the team generate the list of possible solutions?
<--- Score

20. How do you combine the results of individual, and related messages back into a single message?
<--- Score

**21. What results do you get within each

application area of EMM?
<--- Score

22. Is there a small-scale pilot for proposed improvement(s)? What conclusions were drawn from the outcomes of a pilot?
<--- Score

23. What are the overall goals of information risk management?
<--- Score

24. Will the sso solution allow you to integrate your applications simply, or does it require programming?
<--- Score

25. Is there a cost/benefit analysis of optimal solution(s)?
<--- Score

26. What tools were most useful during the improve phase?
<--- Score

27. What is the team's contingency plan for potential problems occurring in implementation?
<--- Score

28. When and how should your organization develop a security policy to address a new situation?
<--- Score

29. Are there newer more affordable network communications solutions that should be tried?

<--- Score

30. How can developers tell the good patterns from the bad patterns?
<--- Score

31. Does the solution need to integrate with other applications?
<--- Score

32. What were the underlying assumptions on the cost-benefit analysis?
<--- Score

33. Which patterns or pattern collections document integration of service based software systems?
<--- Score

34. Will the saas solution need to integrate with your existing enterprise applications?
<--- Score

35. How do you integrate that new solution into your existing business systems?
<--- Score

36. Is the optimal solution selected based on testing and analysis?
<--- Score

37. How can the caller be sure that exactly one receiver will receive the document or perform the call?
<--- Score

38. Is the implementation plan designed?
<--- Score

39. Are improved process ('should be') maps modified based on pilot data and analysis?
<--- Score

40. What are architectural decisions?
<--- Score

41. Is pilot data collected and analyzed?
<--- Score

42. How will the group know that the solution worked?
<--- Score

43. Who will pay for the development and maintenance of the interface/service?
<--- Score

44. How many paying customers does the vendor have for the products being evaluated?
<--- Score

45. What does the 'should be' process map/design look like?
<--- Score

46. How can erm integrate with operational risk management?
<--- Score

47. Describe the design of the pilot and what tests were conducted, if any?
<--- Score

48. What attendant changes will need to be made to ensure that the solution is successful?
<--- Score

49. Do operations in the service interfaces map to transactional boundaries?
<--- Score

50. Is the desired functionality part of the future roadmap in a core or enterprise system?
<--- Score

51. Is a solution implementation plan established, including schedule/work breakdown structure, resources, risk management plan, cost/budget, and control plan?
<--- Score

52. How does the solution remove the key sources of issues discovered in the analyze phase?
<--- Score

53. What tools and techniques were developed that will be useful on future projects?
<--- Score

54. How do you decide which model best suits your organization?
<--- Score

55. What is the unique integration of a jointly engineered solution?
<--- Score

**56. How long has the new technology been in

development?
<--- Score

57. What communications are necessary to support the implementation of the solution?
<--- Score

58. Does the project provide an enterprise wide solution?
<--- Score

59. Do the providers testing solutions integrate with and support the key enterprise applications and technology platforms most critical to your business outcomes?
<--- Score

60. What results do you get within each application area of enterprise models?
<--- Score

61. What error proofing will be done to address some of the discrepancies observed in the 'as is' process?
<--- Score

62. What is rapid application development?
<--- Score

63. Why would you need any other business continuity solutions?
<--- Score

64. Do web services reduce the effort for eai solutions?
<--- Score

65. How can the caller be sure that only one receiver will receive the document or perform the call?

<--- Score

66. Do you need an integrated ERP solution?

<--- Score

67. How will the team or the process owner(s) monitor the implementation plan to see that it is working as intended?

<--- Score

68. Does the bi solution offer ease of integration?

<--- Score

69. Is there a compelling business need to host the solution ourselves?

<--- Score

70. What tools were used to evaluate the potential solutions?

<--- Score

71. What is the implementation plan?

<--- Score

72. Who is initiating the change that will result from the project?

<--- Score

73. Were any criteria developed to assist the team in testing and evaluating potential solutions?

<--- Score

74. What tools were used to tap into the creativity and

encourage 'outside the box' thinking?
<--- Score

75. What are all the applications that would need to be integrated with the eDiscovery solution?
<--- Score

76. Was a pilot designed for the proposed solution(s)?
<--- Score

77. Is customer relationship management integrated to the rest of the ERP solution?
<--- Score

78. What is the configuration of the scanning solution servers?
<--- Score

79. How does a caller get the result of a command message?
<--- Score

80. Is a contingency plan established?
<--- Score

81. What is a good application integration solution?
<--- Score

82. How do you integrate your on premise enterprise document repository with a cloud based business application?
<--- Score

83. How does the solution integrate within existing enterprise systems?

<--- Score

84. What is Enterprise Integration Patterns's impact on utilizing the best solution(s)?
<--- Score

Add up total points for this section:
_____ = Total points for this section

Divided by: _____ (number of statements answered) = _____
Average score for this section

Transfer your score to the Enterprise Integration Patterns Index at the beginning of the Self-Assessment.

CRITERION #6: CONTROL:

INTENT: Implement the practical solution. Maintain the performance and correct possible complications.

In my belief, the answer to this question is clearly defined:

5 Strongly Agree

4 Agree

3 Neutral

2 Disagree

1 Strongly Disagree

1. Who has control over the component?
<--- Score

2. Will any special training be provided for results interpretation?
<--- Score

3. Is there a documented and implemented monitoring plan?

<--- Score

4. Is new knowledge gained imbedded in the response plan?
<--- Score

5. How will new or emerging customer needs/requirements be checked/communicated to orient the process toward meeting the new specifications and continually reducing variation?
<--- Score

6. What key inputs and outputs are being measured on an ongoing basis?
<--- Score

7. Is there a recommended audit plan for routine surveillance inspections of Enterprise Integration Patterns's gains?
<--- Score

8. How do you maintain business standards when adding partners?
<--- Score

9. Is there documentation that will support the successful operation of the improvement?
<--- Score

10. Is knowledge gained on process shared and institutionalized?
<--- Score

11. Is there a transfer of ownership and knowledge to process owner and process team tasked with the responsibilities.

<--- Score

12. What activities must be standardized enterprise wide to support data integration?
<--- Score

13. Who is the Enterprise Integration Patterns process owner?
<--- Score

14. Does the Enterprise Integration Patterns performance meet the customer's requirements?
<--- Score

15. Does the response plan contain a definite closed loop continual improvement scheme (e.g., plan-do-check-act)?
<--- Score

16. Do you have any migration plan from legacy applications?
<--- Score

17. How does the control unit know what to do?
<--- Score

18. What is the primary way your IT organization is currently monitoring/managing enterprise applications?
<--- Score

19. Is there a standardized process?
<--- Score

20. What other areas of the group might benefit from the Enterprise Integration Patterns team's

improvements, knowledge, and learning?
<--- Score

21. How will input, process, and output variables be checked to detect for sub-optimal conditions?
<--- Score

22. How real time is the data that appears on the monitoring dashboard?
<--- Score

23. What should the next improvement project be that is related to Enterprise Integration Patterns?
<--- Score

24. Are there standards available for integration of blockchain applications with enterprise systems?
<--- Score

25. How do you best transmit control information along with a message?
<--- Score

26. How will the process owner and team be able to hold the gains?
<--- Score

27. What are the critical parameters to watch?
<--- Score

28. Are common web service standards supported?
<--- Score

29. How do you plan on communicating the value of big data to your organization?

<--- Score

30. How will the day-to-day responsibilities for monitoring and continual improvement be transferred from the improvement team to the process owner?
<--- Score

31. Does a troubleshooting guide exist or is it needed?
<--- Score

32. Does job training on the documented procedures need to be part of the process team's education and training?
<--- Score

33. What is the basis of your current or planned real time data integration environment?
<--- Score

34. How do you decouple the destination of a message from the sender and maintain central control over the flow of messages?
<--- Score

35. How to monitor the system resources and react on critical situations?
<--- Score

36. Are suggested corrective/restorative actions indicated on the response plan for known causes to problems that might surface?
<--- Score

37. What was learned about budgeting that will help you with future projects?

<--- Score

38. Is there a control plan in place for sustaining improvements (short and long-term)?
<--- Score

39. Is there a need to adopt a new technology that will scale once your needs change?
<--- Score

40. What is the control/monitoring plan?
<--- Score

41. What is the recommended frequency of auditing?
<--- Score

42. Is reporting being used or needed?
<--- Score

43. How will report readings be checked to effectively monitor performance?
<--- Score

44. Have new or revised work instructions resulted?
<--- Score

45. Does your integration process scale to match growth?
<--- Score

46. How will the process owner verify improvement in present and future sigma levels, process capabilities?
<--- Score

47. Are new process steps, standards, and documentation ingrained into normal operations?

<--- Score

48. Are operating procedures consistent?
<--- Score

49. Are there training sessions offered so you can learn more about the system?
<--- Score

50. Is it a free for all or do you have to code control and enforcement into the applications and services, again adding to complexity?
<--- Score

51. How to monitor your organizations of all currently processed messages?
<--- Score

52. Has the improved process and its steps been standardized?
<--- Score

53. What type of standard application does your organization use?
<--- Score

54. How can a client control its transactions with the messaging system?
<--- Score

55. Are documented procedures clear and easy to follow for the operators?
<--- Score

56. Is a response plan established and deployed?
<--- Score

57. Are there documented procedures?
<--- Score

58. Is a response plan in place for when the input, process, or output measures indicate an 'out-of-control' condition?
<--- Score

59. How might the group capture best practices and lessons learned so as to leverage improvements?
<--- Score

60. What quality tools were useful in the control phase?
<--- Score

61. What other systems, operations, processes, and infrastructures (hiring practices, staffing, training, incentives/rewards, metrics/dashboards/scorecards, etc.) need updates, additions, changes, or deletions in order to facilitate knowledge transfer and improvements?
<--- Score

62. How does enterprise architecture fit with strategic systems planning?
<--- Score

63. Is the communication plan being followed by all project personnel?
<--- Score

64. Have you planned your data integration?
<--- Score

Add up total points for this section:
_____ = Total points for this section

Divided by: _____ (number of statements answered) = _____
Average score for this section

Transfer your score to the Enterprise Integration Patterns Index at the beginning of the Self-Assessment.

CRITERION #7: SUSTAIN:

INTENT: Retain the benefits.

In my belief, the answer to this question is clearly defined:

5 Strongly Agree

4 Agree

3 Neutral

2 Disagree

1 Strongly Disagree

1. How do you integrate applications at the logical business layer?
<--- Score

2. When an application sends a message, how can it get a response from the receiver?
<--- Score

3. What is the best way to work with multiple teams of people on large projects?
<--- Score

4. How radical is the new technology under consideration?
<--- Score

5. What path can enterprises take to prepare for secure use of APIs?
<--- Score

6. Should application integration projects utilise workflow technology?
<--- Score

7. How many components are interested in receiving a particular message?
<--- Score

8. How do you determine that application route the messages to the right destination?
<--- Score

9. How can a message consumer select which messages it wants to receive?
<--- Score

10. What is an adequate number of representation elements for request and response messages?
<--- Score

11. What are the patterns that can be used?
<--- Score

12. Is sap getting back into the hosting business?
<--- Score

13. Is the message size relatively small or large?

<--- Score

14. Can you integrate quality management and risk management?
<--- Score

15. Do you intend to build a portfolio of applications that integrate with, and build on, one another?
<--- Score

16. What is the most useful form of information you receive?
<--- Score

17. Which routing capabilities are offered?
<--- Score

18. What is the difference between an ERP system and multiple software applications?
<--- Score

19. Do the viable solutions scale to future needs?
<--- Score

20. How does a sender that receives a reply message know which request the reply belongs to?
<--- Score

21. What approaches can be helpful for companies to accomplish successful business to business IT integration pattern for their short and long term goals?
<--- Score

22. Will the service be shared between several business functions?

<--- Score

23. How can a component avoid receiving unwanted messages?

<--- Score

24. How does the identity provider work?

<--- Score

25. What is the api component framework?

<--- Score

26. What consequences do change and model dependencies have on enterprise models application?

<--- Score

27. How to determining which of the enterprise applications can be moved to cloud architecture?

<--- Score

28. How do you temporally decouple the request from a service consumer and the reply from the service?

<--- Score

29. What do you do when a new technology arrives?

<--- Score

30. What does application support offer your business?

<--- Score

31. Is the current architecture supporting and adding value to your organization?
<--- Score

32. How do you manage enterprise security?
<--- Score

33. How should the various cloud services integrate with the existing enterprise security architecture?
<--- Score

34. What is a vertically integrated information system?
<--- Score

35. Are the applications on premise or cloud based?
<--- Score

36. Have you centrally integrated the enterprise applications?
<--- Score

37. What are microservices, and what are the advantages of adopting a microservices architecture?
<--- Score

38. Which middleware platform should you choose for your next remote service?
<--- Score

39. Are other applications to be integrated?
<--- Score

40. What is driving enterprise integration demand growth?
<--- Score

41. What ever happened to software architecture?
<--- Score

42. How do web services affect integration projects in practice?
<--- Score

43. Where do your applications live?
<--- Score

44. What are the current key technical barriers to information exchange?
<--- Score

45. What distinguishes an integrated set of applications from non integrated applications?
<--- Score

46. Do you know all the contacts a customer has with your organization?
<--- Score

47. What is the architecture and infrastructure for services over time?
<--- Score

48. Which business capabilities will benefit most from cloud applications or hybrid cloud integration?
<--- Score

49. When should a process be art not science?

<--- Score

50. Are the most efficient solutions problem-specific?
<--- Score

51. What can companies get from and other enterprise applications?
<--- Score

52. How many users can share the load at the most bottleneck points?
<--- Score

53. How can a messaging receiver gracefully handle receiving a message that makes no sense?
<--- Score

54. How do you route messages based on a dynamic list of destinations?
<--- Score

55. What is cloud computing all about?
<--- Score

56. What is service oriented architecture?
<--- Score

57. What are the key concerns associated with managing an IS organizations personnel?
<--- Score

58. How much redundancy should there be in the design of the network?
<--- Score

59. Will the consumer receive the message over channel even when messaging system crashes?
<--- Score

60. Why you should extend your SOA for inter organization integration?
<--- Score

61. Is there any way to speed up the process?
<--- Score

62. What are the types for implementing integration pattern?
<--- Score

63. What makes software collaborations different?
<--- Score

64. How are the different information assets linked together?
<--- Score

65. What are the primary reasons for implementing an ERP system?
<--- Score

66. How did you implement your migration strategy?
<--- Score

67. Why might your organization wish to stay in an earlier stage of the long term?
<--- Score

68. How did you get to the point of having disparate, disconnected applications?

<--- Score

69. What percentage of all deployed applications are considered businesscritical?

<--- Score

70. What is application integration?

<--- Score

71. What type of integration mechanisms exists in the application being targeted?

<--- Score

72. What financial commitments must the business make?

<--- Score

73. What is the business value of an Enterprise PaaS?

<--- Score

74. Do you have the optimal project management team structure?

<--- Score

75. Are resources wasted by enhancing applications of low business value?

<--- Score

76. What does successful integration look like?

<--- Score

77. How do design patterns relate to the enterprise?

<--- Score

78. What reference architectures are used for blockchain applications?

<--- Score

79. Which does your organization currently include in its integration strategy?

<--- Score

80. How to design, buy, and test flexible infrastructure?

<--- Score

81. How digital is communication in your organization?

<--- Score

82. How do you application communicate with another using messaging?

<--- Score

83. Which blockchain platforms could be used to create blockchain applications?

<--- Score

84. What is the enterprises expected availability?

<--- Score

85. What other applications do you integrate with or have integrated with in the past?

<--- Score

86. What are the logical patterns enabling enterprise integration?

<--- Score

**87. How does the new authentication method

integrate with the enterprises spectrum of applications?

<--- Score

88. What structural changes occurred in the enterprise?

<--- Score

89. What kind of enterprises do you expect to find?

<--- Score

90. How can messaging be used to invoke a procedure in another application?

<--- Score

91. How do you ensure that exactly one receiver receives a message?

<--- Score

92. Are all business objectives and critical success factors addressed?

<--- Score

93. How is the financial stability of your organization determined?

<--- Score

94. Have the integration goals been met?

<--- Score

95. What is information technology governance?

<--- Score

96. Is cloud based ERP really ready for your business?

<--- Score

97. How do you avoid making services too coarse grained or too fine grained?
<--- Score

98. How do you encapsulate access to the messaging system from the rest of the application?
<--- Score

99. What service versioning mechanism will be used?
<--- Score

100. When do you expect partner integrations?
<--- Score

101. What are the benefits of enterprise integration?
<--- Score

102. What are the usual enterprise applications with which the product is interfaced?
<--- Score

103. How easy is it to get information?
<--- Score

104. What architectures, tools, and applications will be ideal for technology enabled marketing?
<--- Score

105. How do you increase service autonomy and handle temporal concerns?
<--- Score

106. How would your organization support resiliency?
<--- Score

107. Why do customer relationship management applications affect customer satisfaction?
<--- Score

108. What is the most important challenge in managing integration projects?
<--- Score

109. What makes open source an attractive type of purchased software?
<--- Score

110. How to sort the content of a message?
<--- Score

111. Is it possible to have too much information about a customer?
<--- Score

112. How do you reach distributed consensus between services without transactions?
<--- Score

113. Will some workflows be better serviced by mobile devices and smart phones, which are also fully integrated with the real time enterprise application?
<--- Score

114. How many eai implementation attempts were successful prior to project i?
<--- Score

115. How long should old versions of services/operations be available?
<--- Score

116. Do you already have a messaging system on the enterprise tier?
<--- Score

117. How do you split a single message into pieces to be routed individually?
<--- Score

118. How long to keep data and how to manage retention costs?
<--- Score

119. How do you route messages differently?
<--- Score

120. What are the applications in the IT portfolio?
<--- Score

121. Why message oriented middleware?
<--- Score

122. How many operations are in the service?
<--- Score

123. Do you intend to contract for professional services in a separate procurement?
<--- Score

124. How can the authenticity of a message be ensured?
<--- Score

125. Which level of business do you most strongly associate with?
<--- Score

126. How to compress the message content?
<--- Score

127. How does the receiver of a message know where to send the reply message?
<--- Score

128. Does the financial strategy include managing the shared service as your organization?
<--- Score

129. What makes good application integration?
<--- Score

130. How do you build services to handle computationally intense tasks in a scalable manner?
<--- Score

131. How do you call a remote service in a distributed system by looking up the service in a registry?
<--- Score

132. Are there any limitations to the kind/amount of information being integrated?
<--- Score

133. What is enterprise architecture?
<--- Score

134. Can is/it governance contribute for business agility?

<--- Score

135. How important are capabilities in an integration platform?

<--- Score

136. How does business view IT and why?

<--- Score

137. Are you a service stakeholder owned business?

<--- Score

138. Does your organization have an intranet?

<--- Score

139. How to estimate the benefits of an enterprise integration system in monetary terms?

<--- Score

140. How will the data be checked for quality?

<--- Score

141. What role does a key distribution center play in secure channels?

<--- Score

142. What access levels are implemented?

<--- Score

143. Which mobile enterprise applications have maas available?

<--- Score

144. Are the applications used by the business able to integrate with and support new technologies?
<--- Score

145. How does a sender limit how much time can be used to transmit the message?
<--- Score

146. Is the work to date meeting requirements?
<--- Score

147. What works well, and what is still missing?
<--- Score

148. What are semantics in digital systems?
<--- Score

149. What are the benefits and challenges of an integrated enterprise system?
<--- Score

150. What consequences does accuracy of the view have on enterprise models application?
<--- Score

151. What is approximate budget for project?
<--- Score

152. What application version is supported?
<--- Score

153. Which patterns or pattern collections exist that support designing service based software system?
<--- Score

154. Which domain are you working in?

<--- Score

155. Do you send information from multiple related objects?

<--- Score

156. Why take the time to integrate older enterprise systems and applications with other internal and external services?

<--- Score

157. What would an ideal service oriented architecture look like?

<--- Score

158. How can the employees be motivated to use the newly introduced technology?

<--- Score

159. Which interfaces/services to do first?

<--- Score

160. How do you ensure security when working with partners?

<--- Score

161. Which is the architectural role played by each API endpoint and its operations?

<--- Score

162. Do the existing applications/systems have facilities/functionality to support the integration desired?

<--- Score

163. How do you combine multiple messages into a single combined message?

<--- Score

164. How will applications be made available on the execution platform?

<--- Score

165. How does object oriented programming fit into generations?

<--- Score

166. How to know a service has failed?

<--- Score

167. How does the provider know where to send the reply?

<--- Score

168. Are procedures documented for managing Enterprise Integration Patterns risks?

<--- Score

169. How many messages do you buffer?

<--- Score

170. What is agile enterprise integration software?

<--- Score

171. Which additional integration projects might provide value to the business?

<--- Score

172. When was eai first adopted in project is organization?

<--- Score

173. How do you go about importing all that information?
<--- Score

174. How many users will the new system support?
<--- Score

175. What specific programs or types of programs is your organization referring to?
<--- Score

176. Are all business functions included?
<--- Score

177. What applications are used within your organization to support internal/external business services?
<--- Score

178. How do you make applications conform to the common format?
<--- Score

179. What information is typically included in an initial IT project request?
<--- Score

180. How close do the applications being integrated reside to one another?
<--- Score

181. How can an EA help in enterprise integration efforts?
<--- Score

182. Which approaches is most common to use in integrating applications?

<--- Score

183. What makes for good application integration?

<--- Score

184. What kinds of training should you have your teams participate in?

<--- Score

185. Which enterprise servers are to be accessed by the application?

<--- Score

186. Does the product offer message normalization?

<--- Score

187. What challenges do system integration present?

<--- Score

188. Is mes integrated with enterprise applications?

<--- Score

189. How can a message consumer select which messages it wishes to receive?

<--- Score

190. What proportion of enterprise integration barriers are technical?

<--- Score

191. How do you discard unwanted messages?

<--- Score

192. Is project you the first attempt at eai in your organization?

<--- Score

193. Has your current system been modified or customized?

<--- Score

194. How should integration be managed and governed?

<--- Score

195. Are risk management tasks balanced centrally and locally?

<--- Score

196. What is the acceptable amount of coupling between components in different governance zones?

<--- Score

197. What was the approximate budget of the project?

<--- Score

198. Is the Enterprise Integration Patterns solution sustainable?

<--- Score

199. Is the same true of architectural patterns?

<--- Score

200. How do enterprise design patterns relate to

the enterprise?
<--- Score

201. Which interfaces /services to do?
<--- Score

202. How much is your enterprise geographically dispersed?
<--- Score

203. How do you elicit and capture customer feedback and integrate it into an effective customer experience?
<--- Score

204. Are the early projects positioned for success?
<--- Score

205. How many ERP implementation attempts were successful prior to project p?
<--- Score

206. Does management have the right priorities among projects?
<--- Score

207. How will corresponding data be collected?
<--- Score

208. How can the current IT architecture of your organization help in achieving the new services?
<--- Score

209. How do you inspect messages that travel on a point to point channel?
<--- Score

210. Do it projects undertaken flow from an understanding of the business strategy?

<--- Score

211. How is the traditional enterprise IT operating model evolving?

<--- Score

212. Will the cash management system be integrated with other enterprise financial applications?

<--- Score

213. How easy is it to integrate with back end resources or applications?

<--- Score

214. How do you route a message to a number of endpoints at the same time?

<--- Score

215. What are the methods of application integration?

<--- Score

216. How does a message endpoint know when a new message is available?

<--- Score

217. What is the current management/operational personnel attitude?

<--- Score

218. How do you connect to devices so that enterprise applications can communicate with the

devices?
<--- Score

219. Do you integrate labeling with your enterprise applications?
<--- Score

220. Have you integrated the communications platforms with the enterprise applications?
<--- Score

221. What application integration does it offer?
<--- Score

222. Does the subscriber receive the message?
<--- Score

223. How to securely integrate mobile apps to enterprise systems?
<--- Score

224. What are the benefits of applications integration?
<--- Score

225. How do you work with a mixture of hardware, operating systems, and versions?
<--- Score

226. Have many audit professionals and audit organizations adopt an integrated audit approach?
<--- Score

227. How do you keep left over messages on a channel from disturbing tests or running systems?

<--- Score

228. How to verify a messages authenticity, integrity and non repudiation?

<--- Score

229. How can multiple applications work together to exchange information?

<--- Score

230. Have the opportunities for current and forthcoming technologies been fully considered?

<--- Score

231. Do you have enough people assigned to the project?

<--- Score

232. Which types of failures is the system subject to?

<--- Score

233. Why would a consumer want to receive certain messages only?

<--- Score

234. How will an enterprises middleware choices affect its success with packaged software integration?

<--- Score

235. Should message level security be used to protect messages?

<--- Score

236. How is that different or better than

integration on the UI side?

<--- Score

237. What is the end to end error handling strategy across systems?

<--- Score

238. How should the target business and information environment be designed?

<--- Score

239. Which incoming messages belong together?

<--- Score

240. What kind of your organization might choose to have low levels of dependence on IT?

<--- Score

241. Does the structure of the information help you with your tasks?

<--- Score

242. How do you guarantee that your architecture is in fact robust and extensible?

<--- Score

243. How do you integrate applications at the business logic layer?

<--- Score

244. What kind of functional capabilities are provided by the intra enterprise application integration technologies?

<--- Score

245. What is the acceptable length of time for the

system to be down?

<--- Score

246. What are the current segment investments, systems, and resources?

<--- Score

247. What is the difference between a primary key and a unique constraint?

<--- Score

248. What is the clients view of security in IoT?

<--- Score

249. What does the framework consist of?

<--- Score

250. Should you modify an application product?

<--- Score

251. What resources do you allocate for each application area of EMM?

<--- Score

252. What integration approach should be followed?

<--- Score

253. How do other organizations choose the right path and the right balance?

<--- Score

254. Do you use IT to help your customers increase revenues?

<--- Score

255. What application integration exists now?
<--- Score

256. Does the system integrate with supportive technology as interactive voice response systems that operate in multiple languages?
<--- Score

257. What type of dishonest organization are you running?
<--- Score

258. How do you integrate your applications into the same identity space?
<--- Score

259. What is an integrated enterprise system and how did you get here?
<--- Score

260. What better services must be provided by LSPs to remain relevant in market?
<--- Score

261. What do you do to make integration points safer?
<--- Score

262. How should integration disciplines be organized?
<--- Score

263. What is web application integration and why might you use it?
<--- Score

264. What are the current aims of business integration, and what stage has the market reached?

<--- Score

265. How do messages get placed into queues?

<--- Score

266. What kinds of portable IT help employees work more efficiently and effectively?

<--- Score

267. What would be good strategies to minimize coupling between different applications?

<--- Score

268. What are characteristic of legacy system?

<--- Score

269. Do you have the same approach to enterprises?

<--- Score

270. How wraps dissimilar applications?

<--- Score

271. How can an application consume a message when the application is ready?

<--- Score

272. Which applications systems are employed in realizing which business services?

<--- Score

273. Did you find any errors in the information?

<--- Score

274. How to match request and reply messages?
<--- Score

275. Does the application support integration with an enterprise identity management system?
<--- Score

276. Does the it strategy of your organization address application integration with application services?
<--- Score

277. What information is important to communicate?
<--- Score

278. Which sap version and applications do you have?
<--- Score

279. What is the financial soundness of your organization offering the new technology?
<--- Score

280. How might architecture be modified so that it adds more value to your organization?
<--- Score

281. How much time do you spend working on a PC or the central system on the average each day?
<--- Score

282. Are you willing to participate in another shadowing experience in the near future?
<--- Score

283. Is a threat the destruction of the system or destruction/loss/falsification of information?
<--- Score

284. How well are you using your current systems and technologies?
<--- Score

285. Do you offer SSO without modification to the SaaS application or integration with SAML / OAUTH?
<--- Score

286. Which research organizations to partner with businesses to conduct the research for the project?
<--- Score

287. Why is integration important to the enterprise?
<--- Score

288. Who manages supplier risk management in your organization?
<--- Score

289. How does a replier know where to send the reply?
<--- Score

290. Which transformation capabilities are offered?
<--- Score

291. Are web services worth a second look?
<--- Score

292. How do you keep systems updated painlessly?

<--- Score

293. How to detect inactive components like channels or patterns?

<--- Score

294. What is your budget for initial integration efforts?

<--- Score

295. What spurred enterprises growing interest?

<--- Score

296. Are resources wasted by the unnecessary enhancement of applications of low business value?

<--- Score

297. How do you best think about the range of enterprise integration options?

<--- Score

298. What will the messaging system do with a message it cannot deliver?

<--- Score

299. How do you application communicate with another application using messaging?

<--- Score

300. What exactly is message oriented middleware?

<--- Score

301. What is the level of your familiarity with the software/reference?
<--- Score

302. What should the integration allow you to do?
<--- Score

303. How well do the existing systems and services currently support the mission?
<--- Score

304. Will the project be implemented in phases?
<--- Score

305. What type of benefits do you expect enterprise mobile applications will have on your business?
<--- Score

306. How will duplicates be handled in middleware and in the target system?
<--- Score

307. How does business mashups differ from enterprise portals?
<--- Score

308. What is your organization of the team?
<--- Score

309. Can soa finally deliver on the promise of enterprise integration?
<--- Score

310. Do changing technologies really matter?

<--- Score

311. What is the appropriate granularity for the operations in each service interface?
<--- Score

312. Do you use IT to match an existing competitors offerings?
<--- Score

313. What are the benefits of application integration?
<--- Score

314. What is the lifetime remaining for the legacy system?
<--- Score

315. How can the system be recovered if anything happens?
<--- Score

316. Is the remote endpoint able to respond to the request with low latency?
<--- Score

317. What existing applications provide basic capabilities and information?
<--- Score

318. What constitutes a hybrid cloud?
<--- Score

319. What resources do you allocate for each application area of enterprise models?
<--- Score

320. What was your level of involvement in the project?
<--- Score

321. How can the sender make sure that a message will be delivered, even if the messaging system fails?
<--- Score

322. What are provider applications and resources?
<--- Score

323. What services should be built first?
<--- Score

324. Which information resources would you most like to use more?
<--- Score

325. How can a service handle requests reliably?
<--- Score

326. How much is out of the box and how much is through custom integration?
<--- Score

327. What is important at the level of the internal integration of applications?
<--- Score

328. Have a custom API based application for which there is no off the shelf connector?
<--- Score

329. How many eai implementation attempts were unsuccessful prior to project i?
<--- Score

330. How do you delay the sending of a message?
<--- Score

331. What is the acquisition integration timeline?
<--- Score

332. How to select a good alternate path in large peer to peer systems?
<--- Score

333. What systems/processes must you excel at?
<--- Score

334. Will implementing b2b application integration between several enterprises provide a return worthy of the investment?
<--- Score

335. What percent of all applications do you feel is practical to integrate?
<--- Score

336. Does your application include integrated motion?
<--- Score

337. Where should the message be stored before it is forwarded?
<--- Score

338. How long should you wait for a message?
<--- Score

339. What is asynchronous message based integration?

<--- Score

340. What is oracle application integration architecture?

<--- Score

341. How does your organization integrate with systems and applications from their business partners?

<--- Score

342. What existing systems and services are deployed?

<--- Score

343. How do you integrate your on premises application with external business partners?

<--- Score

344. Which subscriptions receive the messages?

<--- Score

345. Why insight for azure iam services?

<--- Score

346. Who will facilitate the team and process?

<--- Score

347. What do you do when someone wants to build a new system?

<--- Score

**348. How will the PKI elements be integrated into

real business applications?
<--- Score

349. How are business roles assigned to employees within your enterprise?
<--- Score

350. Why are software product lines important?
<--- Score

351. What system do you connect to next?
<--- Score

352. How do you route messages based on a static or dynamic list of destinations?
<--- Score

353. How does a message get to its destination?
<--- Score

354. What are the common approaches of integration in your team?
<--- Score

355. What are the characteristic of network hidden by stream abstraction?
<--- Score

356. Have all stakeholders been considered?
<--- Score

357. How satisfied are people with the current system?
<--- Score

**358. How many ERP implementation attempts

were unsuccessful prior to project p?

<--- Score

359. How will enterprises and vendors respond to the growing tendency to package multiple platform products into integrated suites?

<--- Score

360. What values are generated for individuals and your organization?

<--- Score

361. Why should enterprise applications have their own interface?

<--- Score

362. What alternative responses are available to manage risk?

<--- Score

363. How can a message receiver deal with duplicate messages?

<--- Score

364. What is the tentative timeline for execution of the project?

<--- Score

365. What assumptions are made about the solution and approach?

<--- Score

366. What barriers do you see in putting integration platform into production?

<--- Score

367. How to start scheduling from the last message or action after system restart?
<--- Score

368. Is the information clearly presented?
<--- Score

369. What is the best way to integrate with all your internal applications, as well as all of your customer and trading partner applications?
<--- Score

370. How do you organize your Enterprise Architecture functions and roles to support an SOA?
<--- Score

371. Do you use IT to differentiate your products/services?
<--- Score

372. How to handle failed or timed out requests or short circuits constructively?
<--- Score

373. Does the tool integrate with other enterprise applications or custom applications?
<--- Score

374. Does your service have partners?
<--- Score

375. What is it about integration of IT applications that have value to your organization?
<--- Score

376. What is an ideal time to implement the application?

<--- Score

377. How do you get a stream of related and out of sequence messages back into the correct order?

<--- Score

378. What does application containment do?

<--- Score

379. What is your organizations business effectiveness?

<--- Score

380. What integration tools does the vendor provide?

<--- Score

381. How do you sort the body of a message?

<--- Score

382. How many and which operating systems will your organization support?

<--- Score

383. Does your organization support a marketplace of current integrations or enhancement applications?

<--- Score

384. What is the execution platform for the applications?

<--- Score

385. What is service oriented architecture, and

how does it relate to Web services?

<--- Score

386. How do you ensure ordering of messages?

<--- Score

387. Do you run your enterprise applications on the platform?

<--- Score

388. What is the benefits of online infrastructure?

<--- Score

389. Is project p the first attempt at ERP in your organization?

<--- Score

390. What is contained in the mix of applications?

<--- Score

391. What is knowledge management, and what is a knowledge management system?

<--- Score

392. What is integration platform as a service?

<--- Score

393. Why is it important for your organization to have an information security policy?

<--- Score

394. How can a remote procedure be called as a message?

<--- Score

**395. How can multiple applications work together

and exchange information?

<--- Score

396. How to decompress message content?

<--- Score

397. Is the message size small or large?

<--- Score

398. What is the right size for a microservice?

<--- Score

399. Do you integrate and parse complex application logs?

<--- Score

400. Which business applications should move to the cloud first?

<--- Score

401. How many exchange integrated applications are currently in use?

<--- Score

402. What type of integration mechanisms exists in the application?

<--- Score

403. How does an information vision differ from an IT architecture?

<--- Score

404. What about integration to existing and other cloud applications?

<--- Score

405. Will the user have access for invoking the custom user interface?

<--- Score

406. Which types of applications are other organizations integrating with labeling?

<--- Score

407. What is enterprise content management?

<--- Score

408. Why is object technology valuable?

<--- Score

409. How does the receiver of a request message know where to send the reply message?

<--- Score

410. Which factors apply to the business function or activity?

<--- Score

411. Should a service registry be used?

<--- Score

412. What will it take to implement successful, real time integration in mainstream enterprises?

<--- Score

413. What are the trends in enterprise adoption, use and best practices for integration middleware, and how will its technologies, products, vendors and markets evolve?

<--- Score

**414. Is the business ready for additional

customers?

<--- Score

415. What is the difference between design patterns and architectural patterns?

<--- Score

416. Can the platform connect to all existing applications?

<--- Score

417. What is service oriented integration?

<--- Score

418. What is your idea of the ideal project?

<--- Score

419. When do you send the aggregate message?

<--- Score

420. What about the other applications?

<--- Score

421. What are the patterns available for message transformation?

<--- Score

422. Did the message get onto the queue?

<--- Score

423. What should the channel do once it receives a message from a client?

<--- Score

424. Do you consider dedicated queues for specific workers?

<--- Score

425. Where does spring integration fit in?
<--- Score

426. What are the trends in enterprise adoption, use and best practices for PaaS, and how will its technologies, products, vendors and markets evolve?
<--- Score

427. Can an email gateway be considered a service?
<--- Score

428. How satisfied are people with each of the current systems?
<--- Score

429. What is plm and why is it important to your organizations business?
<--- Score

430. What knowledge or experience is required?
<--- Score

431. How to choose between app integration patterns?
<--- Score

432. What is your organization license?
<--- Score

**433. How will enterprises buy, deploy and integrate application platform technology as vendors shift their traditional delivery and

product packaging models?
<--- Score

434. What is the difference between service orientation and SOA?
<--- Score

435. Do your current applications limit your ability to deliver new products or business services?
<--- Score

436. Has your organization allocated funding for the Enterprise Applications Managed Services yet?
<--- Score

437. Can oracle enterprise server be used for real time authorization in enterprise applications?
<--- Score

438. How can a component avoid receiving uninteresting messages?
<--- Score

439. Why integrate content management into applications?
<--- Score

440. Which approach, new software, or open source automation framework, is best?
<--- Score

441. What is an Application Business Connector Service?
<--- Score

442. Are the risks fully understood, reasonable

and manageable?

<--- Score

443. What is their strategy for API management?

<--- Score

444. Do cloud applications represent a new silo?

<--- Score

445. Which human users and systems will the cloud infrastructure be exposed to?

<--- Score

446. What are the perceived benefits of applications integration people associate with enterprise systems?

<--- Score

447. Why has the IS leadership role in organizations become so important?

<--- Score

448. What is web clipping and why might you use it?

<--- Score

449. How can it facilitate integration across your entire enterprise?

<--- Score

450. Do you feel application integration is desirable or undesirable?

<--- Score

451. Are you a service disabled stakeholder owned business or a stakeholder owned business?

<--- Score

452. How do you enable a service consumer to interact with a service simply?

<--- Score

453. How does the consumer know when a new message is available?

<--- Score

454. How can a messages authenticity, integrity and non repudiation be verified?

<--- Score

455. Who are their customers or suppliers?

<--- Score

456. When was the integration or iPaaS product brought to market?

<--- Score

457. How do smart enterprises resolve the challenges?

<--- Score

458. What are the system strategies for exception handling and fault recovery?

<--- Score

459. How to store messages confidential?

<--- Score

460. Which web services protocols can be used?

<--- Score

461. Which component determines whether a

message should be handled synchronously or asynchronously?

<--- Score

462. How far will international economic integration go?

<--- Score

463. How do conventional application packages and ERP packages differ?

<--- Score

464. How do you get a stream of related, and out of sequence, messages back into the correct order?

<--- Score

465. How does a component avoid receiving uninteresting messages?

<--- Score

466. How do you get started designing with patterns?

<--- Score

467. How do you track monthly usage for subscription based services?

<--- Score

468. How to stay informed about the systems sanity?

<--- Score

469. How satisfied are you with the current application integration at your organization?

<--- Score

470. What are enterprise design patterns?
<--- Score

471. Are the key business and technology risks being managed?
<--- Score

472. Why is enterprise integration so difficult?
<--- Score

473. How do you see the information systems role with respect to the business purpose?
<--- Score

474. What are the trends in enterprise adoption, use and best practices for platform middleware, and how will its technologies, products, vendors and markets evolve?
<--- Score

475. Are there other strategic factors which present a barrier to integration?
<--- Score

476. How close to the scheduled completion date was the project actually finished?
<--- Score

477. What are the different operating systems being used currently?
<--- Score

478. How long will it take the operation to complete in the application?
<--- Score

479. How likely are you to recommend application integration to others?

<--- Score

480. What have non adopters used to deliver the application integrations already done?

<--- Score

481. Who will review the application?

<--- Score

482. Why do many organizations find it difficult to implement an ERP system?

<--- Score

483. What are the processes for audit reporting and management?

<--- Score

Add up total points for this section:
_____ = Total points for this section

Divided by: _____ (number of statements answered) = _____
Average score for this section

Transfer your score to the Enterprise Integration Patterns Index at the beginning of the Self-Assessment.

Enterprise Integration Patterns and Managing Projects, Criteria for Project Managers:

1.0 Initiating Process Group: Enterprise Integration Patterns

1. Are stakeholders properly informed about the status of the Enterprise Integration Patterns project?

2. How well did the chosen processes fit the needs of the Enterprise Integration Patterns project?

3. Are you just doing busywork to pass the time?

4. In which Enterprise Integration Patterns project management process group is the detailed Enterprise Integration Patterns project budget created?

5. Were resources available as planned?

6. What will you do to minimize the impact should a risk event occur?

7. Are identified risks being monitored properly, are new risks arising during the Enterprise Integration Patterns project or are foreseen risks occurring?

8. Who is performing the work of the Enterprise Integration Patterns project?

9. What communication items need improvement?

10. When will the Enterprise Integration Patterns project be done?

11. What areas does the group agree are the biggest success on the Enterprise Integration Patterns project?

12. Do you know the Enterprise Integration Patterns projects goal, purpose and objectives?

13. What do you need to do?

14. Who supports, improves, and oversees standardized processes related to the Enterprise Integration Patterns projects program?

15. At which cmmi level are software processes documented, standardized, and integrated into a standard to-be practiced process for your organization?

16. Measurable - are the targets measurable?

17. Professionals want to know what is expected from them what are the deliverables?

18. What areas were overlooked on this Enterprise Integration Patterns project?

19. The process to Manage Stakeholders is part of which process group?

20. What are the overarching issues of your organization?

1.1 Project Charter: Enterprise Integration Patterns

21. Market – identify products market, including whether it is outside of the objective: what is the purpose of the program or Enterprise Integration Patterns project?

22. What is in it for you?

23. Why use a Enterprise Integration Patterns project charter?

24. What goes into your Enterprise Integration Patterns project Charter?

25. Assumptions: what factors, for planning purposes, are you considering to be true?

26. Who manages integration?

27. What changes can you make to improve?

28. Dependent Enterprise Integration Patterns projects: what Enterprise Integration Patterns projects must be underway or completed before this Enterprise Integration Patterns project can be successful?

29. When?

30. Who are the stakeholders?

31. Name and describe the elements that deal with providing the detail?

32. What are the assigned resources?

33. How do you manage integration?

34. How will you know that a change is an improvement?

35. Who will take notes, document decisions?

36. Will this replace an existing product?

37. When is a charter needed?

38. Why do you need to manage scope?

39. Who is the sponsor?

40. Why have you chosen the aim you have set forth?

1.2 Stakeholder Register: Enterprise Integration Patterns

41. What & Why?

42. What opportunities exist to provide communications?

43. How big is the gap?

44. How should employers make voices heard?

45. How will reports be created?

46. What is the power of the stakeholder?

47. Who wants to talk about Security?

48. How much influence do they have on the Enterprise Integration Patterns project?

49. Is your organization ready for change?

50. What are the major Enterprise Integration Patterns project milestones requiring communications or providing communications opportunities?

51. Who is managing stakeholder engagement?

1.3 Stakeholder Analysis Matrix: Enterprise Integration Patterns

52. Marketing - reach, distribution, awareness?

53. What actions can be taken to reduce or mitigate risk?

54. Volumes, production, economies?

55. What do people from other organizations see as your organizations weaknesses?

56. Legislative effects?

57. Who will be responsible for managing the outcome?

58. Identify the stakeholders levels most frequently used –or at least sought– in your Enterprise Integration Patterns projects and for which purpose?

59. Has there been a similar initiative in the region?

60. How will the stakeholder directly benefit from the Enterprise Integration Patterns project and how will this affect the stakeholders motivation?

61. How much do resources cost?

62. Partnership opportunities/synergies?

63. How do rules, behaviors affect stakes?

64. Political effects?

65. What is the stakeholders power and status in relation to the Enterprise Integration Patterns project?

66. Are you going to weigh the stakeholders?

67. What is your organizations competitors doing?

68. Disadvantages of proposition?

69. Cultural, attitudinal, behavioural?

70. Geographical, export, import?

71. What should thwe organizations stakeholders avoid?

2.0 Planning Process Group: Enterprise Integration Patterns

72. Why is it important to determine activity sequencing on Enterprise Integration Patterns projects?

73. Does it make any difference if you are successful?

74. If you are late, will anybody notice?

75. How well defined and documented are the Enterprise Integration Patterns project management processes you chose to use?

76. Will the products created live up to the necessary quality?

77. In which Enterprise Integration Patterns project management process group is the detailed Enterprise Integration Patterns project budget created?

78. Do the partners have sufficient financial capacity to keep up the benefits produced by the programme?

79. Explanation: is what the Enterprise Integration Patterns project intents to solve a hard question?

80. On which process should team members spend the most time?

81. How well did the chosen processes fit the needs of the Enterprise Integration Patterns project?

82. Does the program have follow-up mechanisms (to verify the quality of the products, punctuality of delivery, etc.) to measure progress in the achievement of the envisaged results?

83. To what extent is the program helping to influence your organizations policy framework?

84. You did your readings, yes?

85. Are work methodologies, financial instruments, etc. shared among departments, organizations and Enterprise Integration Patterns projects?

86. How well will the chosen processes produce the expected results?

87. To what extent has a PMO contributed to raising the quality of the design of the Enterprise Integration Patterns project?

88. What input will you be required to provide the Enterprise Integration Patterns project team?

89. Is the schedule for the set products being met?

90. Why do it Enterprise Integration Patterns projects fail?

2.1 Project Management Plan: Enterprise Integration Patterns

91. Are there any Client staffing expectations?

92. What are the constraints?

93. Are there any scope changes proposed for a previously authorized Enterprise Integration Patterns project?

94. What are the known stakeholder requirements?

95. Is there anything you would now do differently on your Enterprise Integration Patterns project based on past experience?

96. What would you do differently?

97. How do you organize the costs in the Enterprise Integration Patterns project management plan?

98. What went right?

99. Is the budget realistic?

100. Was the peer (technical) review of the cost estimates duly coordinated with the cost estimate center of expertise and addressed in the review documentation and certification?

101. If the Enterprise Integration Patterns project is complex or scope is specialized, do you have

appropriate and/or qualified staff available to perform the tasks?

102. What data/reports/tools/etc. do program managers need?

103. Do there need to be organizational changes?

104. How well are you able to manage your risk?

105. What does management expect of PMs?

106. Did the planning effort collaborate to develop solutions that integrate expertise, policies, programs, and Enterprise Integration Patterns projects across entities?

107. When is the Enterprise Integration Patterns project management plan created?

108. Is the appropriate plan selected based on your organizations objectives and evaluation criteria expressed in Principles and Guidelines policies?

109. If the Enterprise Integration Patterns project management plan is a comprehensive document that guides you in Enterprise Integration Patterns project execution and control, then what should it NOT contain?

2.2 Scope Management Plan: Enterprise Integration Patterns

110. Are trade-offs between accepting the risk and mitigating the risk identified?

111. What should you drop in order to add something new?

112. Knowing the health of the Enterprise Integration Patterns project – What is the status?

113. Will anyone else be involved in verifying the deliverables?

114. Has a sponsor been identified?

115. Are there any windfall benefits that would accrue to the Enterprise Integration Patterns project sponsor or other parties?

116. What is the relative power of the Enterprise Integration Patterns project manager?

117. Is the communication plan being followed?

118. When is corrective or preventative action required?

119. Is there any form of automated support for Issues Management?

120. Has a provision been made to reassess Enterprise

Integration Patterns project risks at various Enterprise Integration Patterns project stages?

121. Alignment to strategic goals & objectives?

122. Is it standard practice to formally commit stakeholders to the Enterprise Integration Patterns project via agreements?

123. Does the detailed work plan match the complexity of tasks with the capabilities of personnel?

124. Is there a Enterprise Integration Patterns project organization chart showing the reporting relationships and responsibilities for each position?

125. Pop quiz – which are the same inputs as in scope planning?

126. Has the Enterprise Integration Patterns project manager been identified?

127. Deliverables -are the deliverables tangible and verifiable?

128. Do you have the reasons why the changes to your organizational systems and capabilities are required?

129. Are tasks tracked by hours?

2.3 Requirements Management Plan: Enterprise Integration Patterns

130. Do you have an appropriate arrangement for meetings?

131. When and how will a requirements baseline be established in this Enterprise Integration Patterns project?

132. Subject to change control?

133. How detailed should the Enterprise Integration Patterns project get?

134. The wbs is developed as part of a joint planning session. and how do you know that youhave done this right?

135. How do you know that you have done this right?

136. Will you document changes to requirements?

137. Are all the stakeholders ready for the transition into the user community?

138. Is there formal agreement on who has authority to request a change in requirements?

139. Who will finally present the work or product(s) for acceptance?

140. Did you provide clear and concise specifications?

141. Who will do the reporting and to whom will reports be delivered?

142. Is requirements work dependent on any other specific Enterprise Integration Patterns project or non-Enterprise Integration Patterns project activities (e.g. funding, approvals, procurement)?

143. Should you include sub-activities?

144. Why manage requirements?

145. Who has the authority to reject Enterprise Integration Patterns project requirements?

146. Have stakeholders been instructed in the Change Control process?

147. Who will initially review the Enterprise Integration Patterns project work or products to ensure it meets the applicable acceptance criteria?

148. How will requirements be managed?

149. Will the contractors involved take full responsibility?

2.4 Requirements Documentation: Enterprise Integration Patterns

150. How do you get the user to tell you what they want?

151. Is the requirement realistically testable?

152. Has requirements gathering uncovered information that would necessitate changes?

153. What are current process problems?

154. Verifiability. can the requirements be checked?

155. What facilities must be supported by the system?

156. How to document system requirements?

157. Completeness. are all functions required by the customer included?

158. What will be the integration problems?

159. What if the system wasn t implemented?

160. Is new technology needed?

161. Basic work/business process; high-level, what is being touched?

162. What happens when requirements are wrong?

163. Where do you define what is a customer, what are the attributes of customer?

164. How much testing do you need to do to prove that your system is safe?

165. How do you know when a Requirement is accurate enough?

166. Can the requirements be checked?

167. What is the risk associated with the technology?

168. Validity. does the system provide the functions which best support the customers needs?

169. Do your constraints stand?

2.5 Requirements Traceability Matrix: Enterprise Integration Patterns

170. Why use a WBS?

171. Do you have a clear understanding of all subcontracts in place?

172. What is the WBS?

173. Describe the process for approving requirements so they can be added to the traceability matrix and Enterprise Integration Patterns project work can be performed. Will the Enterprise Integration Patterns project requirements become approved in writing?

174. What are the chronologies, contingencies, consequences, criteria?

175. How will it affect the stakeholders personally in career?

176. How do you manage scope?

177. Will you use a Requirements Traceability Matrix?

178. How small is small enough?

179. Why do you manage scope?

180. Is there a requirements traceability process in place?

181. What percentage of Enterprise Integration Patterns projects are producing traceability matrices between requirements and other work products?

2.6 Project Scope Statement: Enterprise Integration Patterns

182. Is the Enterprise Integration Patterns project organization documented and on file?

183. Have you been able to easily identify success criteria and create objective measurements for each of the Enterprise Integration Patterns project scopes goal statements?

184. Where and how does the team fit within your organization structure?

185. Relevant - ask yourself can you get there; why are you doing this Enterprise Integration Patterns project?

186. If the scope changes, what will the impact be to your Enterprise Integration Patterns project in terms of duration, cost, quality, or any other important areas of the Enterprise Integration Patterns project?

187. Will the qa related information be reported regularly as part of the status reporting mechanisms?

188. What are the major deliverables of the Enterprise Integration Patterns project?

189. Any new risks introduced or old risks impacted. Are there issues that could affect the existing requirements for the result, service, or product if the scope changes?

190. Once its defined, what is the stability of the Enterprise Integration Patterns project scope?

191. Are there specific processes you will use to evaluate and approve/reject changes?

192. Who will you recommend approve the change, and when do you recommend the change reviews occur?

193. Elements of scope management that deal with concept development ?

194. What is a process you might recommend to verify the accuracy of the research deliverable?

195. Is the change control process documented and on file?

196. Which risks does the Enterprise Integration Patterns project focus on?

197. Will you need a statement of work?

198. Will this process be communicated to the customer and Enterprise Integration Patterns project team?

199. If there is an independent oversight contractor, have they signed off on the Enterprise Integration Patterns project Plan?

2.7 Assumption and Constraint Log: Enterprise Integration Patterns

200. Are there processes in place to ensure internal consistency between the source code components?

201. Are there processes defining how software will be developed including development methods, overall timeline for development, software product standards, and traceability?

202. Is the definition of the Enterprise Integration Patterns project scope clear; what needs to be accomplished?

203. What strengths do you have?

204. After observing execution of process, is it in compliance with the documented Plan?

205. Does the document/deliverable meet all requirements (for example, statement of work) specific to this deliverable?

206. Do you know what your customers expectations are regarding this process?

207. Does a specific action and/or state that is known to violate security policy occur?

208. Do documented requirements exist for all critical components and areas, including technical, business, interfaces, performance, security and conversion

requirements?

209. Should factors be unpredictable over time?

210. Is there documentation of system capability requirements, data requirements, environment requirements, security requirements, and computer and hardware requirements?

211. How do you design an auditing system?

212. Are there procedures in place to effectively manage interdependencies with other Enterprise Integration Patterns projects / systems?

213. Has a Enterprise Integration Patterns project Communications Plan been developed?

214. What worked well?

215. Is there a Steering Committee in place?

216. What is positive about the current process?

217. Does the Enterprise Integration Patterns project have a formal Enterprise Integration Patterns project Plan?

218. How relevant is this attribute to this Enterprise Integration Patterns project or audit?

219. Have all necessary approvals been obtained?

2.8 Work Breakdown Structure: Enterprise Integration Patterns

220. Why is it useful?

221. What is the probability that the Enterprise Integration Patterns project duration will exceed xx weeks?

222. When do you stop?

223. Is the work breakdown structure (wbs) defined and is the scope of the Enterprise Integration Patterns project clear with assigned deliverable owners?

224. What is the probability of completing the Enterprise Integration Patterns project in less that xx days?

225. Do you need another level?

226. How big is a work-package?

227. When would you develop a Work Breakdown Structure?

228. Where does it take place?

229. Is it a change in scope?

230. How much detail?

231. How will you and your Enterprise Integration

Patterns project team define the Enterprise Integration Patterns projects scope and work breakdown structure?

232. Why would you develop a Work Breakdown Structure?

233. Can you make it?

234. Who has to do it?

235. When does it have to be done?

236. What has to be done?

2.9 WBS Dictionary: Enterprise Integration Patterns

237. What is the goal?

238. Are retroactive changes to budgets for completed work specifically prohibited in an established procedure, and is this procedure adhered to?

239. Contractor financial periods; for example, annual?

240. Are there procedures for monitoring action items and corrective actions to the point of resolution and are corresponding procedures being followed?

241. Budgets assigned to major functional organizations?

242. Evaluate the performance of operating organizations?

243. Does the contractors system provide for determination of price variance by comparing planned Vs actual commitments?

244. Identify potential or actual overruns and underruns?

245. Contemplated overhead expenditure for each period based on the best information currently available?

246. Wbs elements contractually specified for reporting of status to you (lowest level only)?

247. Are the rates for allocating costs from each indirect cost pool to contracts updated as necessary to ensure a realistic monthly allocation of indirect costs without significant year-end adjustments?

248. Are work packages reasonably short in time duration or do they have adequate objective indicators/milestones to minimize subjectivity of the in process work evaluation?

249. Are overhead cost budgets established for each organization which has authority to incur overhead costs?

250. Knowledgeable Enterprise Integration Patterns projections of future performance?

251. Are current budgets resulting from changes to the authorized work and/or internal replanning, reconcilable to original budgets for specified reporting items?

252. What size should a work package be?

253. Are data being used by managers in an effective manner to ascertain Enterprise Integration Patterns project or functional status, to identify reasons or significant variance, and to initiate appropriate corrective action?

254. Are estimates of costs at completion generated in a rational, consistent manner?

255. Are the latest revised estimates of costs at completion compared with the established budgets at appropriate levels and causes of variances identified?

2.10 Schedule Management Plan: Enterprise Integration Patterns

256. Can be realistically shortened (the duration of subsequent tasks)?

257. Are mitigation strategies identified?

258. Is the critical path valid?

259. Is documentation created for communication with the suppliers and Vendors?

260. Does the ims reflect accurate current status and credible start/finish forecasts for all to-go tasks and milestones?

261. List all schedule constraints here. Must the Enterprise Integration Patterns project be complete by a specified date?

262. Are scheduled deliverables actually delivered?

263. Are the key elements of a Enterprise Integration Patterns project Charter present?

264. Have all unresolved risks been documented?

265. Are cause and effect determined for risks when they occur?

266. Have Enterprise Integration Patterns project management standards and procedures been

identified / established and documented?

267. Are vendor contract reports, reviews and visits conducted periodically?

268. Does the schedule have reasonable float?

269. After initial schedule development, will the schedule be reviewed and validated by the Enterprise Integration Patterns project team?

270. Is there anything planned that does not need to be here?

271. Were Enterprise Integration Patterns project team members involved in the development of activity & task decomposition?

272. Are there any activities or deliverables being added or gold-plated that could be dropped or scaled back without falling short of the original requirement?

273. Is the assigned Enterprise Integration Patterns project manager a PMP (Certified Enterprise Integration Patterns project manager) and experienced?

2.11 Activity List: Enterprise Integration Patterns

274. What are the critical bottleneck activities?

275. How will it be performed?

276. What is your organizations history in doing similar activities?

277. How much slack is available in the Enterprise Integration Patterns project?

278. How difficult will it be to do specific activities on this Enterprise Integration Patterns project?

279. Are the required resources available or need to be acquired?

280. What are you counting on?

281. Where will it be performed?

282. How detailed should a Enterprise Integration Patterns project get?

283. What did not go as well?

284. How should ongoing costs be monitored to try to keep the Enterprise Integration Patterns project within budget?

285. How can the Enterprise Integration Patterns

project be displayed graphically to better visualize the activities?

286. What is the probability the Enterprise Integration Patterns project can be completed in xx weeks?

287. What went wrong?

288. When will the work be performed?

289. In what sequence?

290. Who will perform the work?

2.12 Activity Attributes: Enterprise Integration Patterns

291. What is missing?

292. How else could the items be grouped?

293. How do you manage time?

294. How difficult will it be to do specific activities on this Enterprise Integration Patterns project?

295. Resources to accomplish the work?

296. What conclusions/generalizations can you draw from this?

297. Resource is assigned to?

298. Where else does it apply?

299. Activity: what is In the Bag?

300. Does your organization of the data change its meaning?

301. Have constraints been applied to the start and finish milestones for the phases?

302. Time for overtime?

303. Is there a trend during the year?

304. Would you consider either of corresponding activities an outlier?

305. Can more resources be added?

306. Were there other ways you could have organized the data to achieve similar results?

307. What is the general pattern here?

308. Have you identified the Activity Leveling Priority code value on each activity?

2.13 Milestone List: Enterprise Integration Patterns

309. What specific improvements did you make to the Enterprise Integration Patterns project proposal since the previous time?

310. What are your competitors vulnerabilities?

311. Continuity, supply chain robustness?

312. Can you derive how soon can the whole Enterprise Integration Patterns project finish?

313. Milestone pages should display the UserID of the person who added the milestone. Does a report or query exist that provides this audit information?

314. Gaps in capabilities?

315. What date will the task finish?

316. Timescales, deadlines and pressures?

317. How late can each activity be finished and started?

318. How will you get the word out to customers?

319. Loss of key staff?

320. Obstacles faced?

321. Who will manage the Enterprise Integration Patterns project on a day-to-day basis?

322. Own known vulnerabilities?

323. Identify critical paths (one or more) and which activities are on the critical path?

324. How difficult will it be to do specific activities on this Enterprise Integration Patterns project?

325. Competitive advantages?

326. What has been done so far?

2.14 Network Diagram: Enterprise Integration Patterns

327. Where do you schedule uncertainty time?

328. Why must you schedule milestones, such as reviews, throughout the Enterprise Integration Patterns project?

329. Planning: who, how long, what to do?

330. What activity must be completed immediately before this activity can start?

331. How confident can you be in your milestone dates and the delivery date?

332. Are the required resources available?

333. If a current contract exists, can you provide the vendor name, contract start, and contract expiration date?

334. Are you on time?

335. What is the lowest cost to complete this Enterprise Integration Patterns project in xx weeks?

336. What activities must follow this activity?

337. What must be completed before an activity can be started?

338. Review the logical flow of the network diagram. Take a look at which activities you have first and then sequence the activities. Do they make sense?

339. If x is long, what would be the completion time if you break x into two parallel parts of y weeks and z weeks?

340. What is the completion time?

341. Where do schedules come from?

342. Are the gantt chart and/or network diagram updated periodically and used to assess the overall Enterprise Integration Patterns project timetable?

343. What are the Key Success Factors?

344. What to do and When?

345. What controls the start and finish of a job?

2.15 Activity Resource Requirements: Enterprise Integration Patterns

346. Which logical relationship does the PDM use most often?

347. What are constraints that you might find during the Human Resource Planning process?

348. Anything else?

349. How do you handle petty cash?

350. What is the Work Plan Standard?

351. Other support in specific areas?

352. Are there unresolved issues that need to be addressed?

353. Why do you do that?

354. Organizational Applicability?

355. When does monitoring begin?

356. Do you use tools like decomposition and rolling-wave planning to produce the activity list and other outputs?

357. How many signatures do you require on a check and does this match what is in your policy and procedures?

2.16 Resource Breakdown Structure: Enterprise Integration Patterns

358. What is the primary purpose of the human resource plan?

359. What defines a successful Enterprise Integration Patterns project?

360. How difficult will it be to do specific activities on this Enterprise Integration Patterns project?

361. What is each stakeholders desired outcome for the Enterprise Integration Patterns project?

362. Goals for the Enterprise Integration Patterns project. What is each stakeholders desired outcome for the Enterprise Integration Patterns project?

363. How should the information be delivered?

364. Any changes from stakeholders?

365. What can you do to improve productivity?

366. What are the requirements for resource data?

367. What defines a successful Enterprise Integration Patterns project?

368. Changes based on input from stakeholders?

369. How can this help you with team building?

370. What is the purpose of assigning and documenting responsibility?

371. When do they need the information?

372. Who will be used as a Enterprise Integration Patterns project team member?

373. Which resources should be in the resource pool?

374. What is the difference between % Complete and % work?

375. The list could probably go on, but, the thing that you would most like to know is, How long & How much?

2.17 Activity Duration Estimates: Enterprise Integration Patterns

376. What tasks can take place concurrently?

377. What type of contract was used and why?

378. Are Enterprise Integration Patterns project records organized, maintained, and assessable by Enterprise Integration Patterns project team members?

379. Enterprise Integration Patterns project has three critical paths. Which BEST describes how this affects the Enterprise Integration Patterns project?

380. Is a contract developed which obligates the seller and the buyer?

381. Do you think Enterprise Integration Patterns project managers of large information technology Enterprise Integration Patterns projects need strong technical skills?

382. What is the critical path for this Enterprise Integration Patterns project and how long is it?

383. What distinguishes one organization from another in this area?

384. Are time, scope, cost, and quality monitored throughout the Enterprise Integration Patterns project?

385. How can you use Microsoft Enterprise Integration Patterns project and Excel to assist in Enterprise Integration Patterns project risk management?

386. Are procurement documents used to solicit accurate and complete proposals from prospective sellers?

387. How can others help Enterprise Integration Patterns project managers understand your organizational context for Enterprise Integration Patterns projects?

388. What steps did your organization take to earn this prestigious quality award?

389. Does a process exist to identify Enterprise Integration Patterns project roles, responsibilities and reporting relationships?

390. Is risk identification completed regularly throughout the Enterprise Integration Patterns project?

391. Are Enterprise Integration Patterns project management tools and techniques consistently applied throughout all Enterprise Integration Patterns projects?

392. Briefly describe some key events in the history of Enterprise Integration Patterns project management. What Enterprise Integration Patterns project was the first to use modern Enterprise Integration Patterns project management?

393. Is a work breakdown structure created to organize and to confirm the scope of each Enterprise Integration Patterns project?

394. Are Enterprise Integration Patterns project costs tracked in the general ledger?

2.18 Duration Estimating Worksheet: Enterprise Integration Patterns

395. What is the total time required to complete the Enterprise Integration Patterns project if no delays occur?

396. What is next?

397. What questions do you have?

398. Small or large Enterprise Integration Patterns project?

399. How can the Enterprise Integration Patterns project be displayed graphically to better visualize the activities?

400. What info is needed?

401. What utility impacts are there?

402. Can the Enterprise Integration Patterns project be constructed as planned?

403. Do any colleagues have experience with your organization and/or RFPs?

404. What is cost and Enterprise Integration Patterns project cost management?

405. Done before proceeding with this activity or what can be done concurrently?

406. What is your role?

407. When, then?

408. Is the Enterprise Integration Patterns project responsive to community need?

409. Value pocket identification & quantification what are value pockets?

410. Why estimate time and cost?

411. How should ongoing costs be monitored to try to keep the Enterprise Integration Patterns project within budget?

412. When do the individual activities need to start and finish?

413. Is this operation cost effective?

2.19 Project Schedule: Enterprise Integration Patterns

414. Is infrastructure setup part of your Enterprise Integration Patterns project?

415. Master Enterprise Integration Patterns project schedule?

416. If you can not fix it, how do you do it differently?

417. Verify that the update is accurate. Are all remaining durations correct?

418. Understand the constraints used in preparing the schedule. Are activities connected because logic dictates the order in which others occur?

419. Is Enterprise Integration Patterns project work proceeding in accordance with the original Enterprise Integration Patterns project schedule?

420. Is the Enterprise Integration Patterns project schedule available for all Enterprise Integration Patterns project team members to review?

421. Month Enterprise Integration Patterns project take?

422. Why is software Enterprise Integration Patterns project disaster so common?

423. Why do you think schedule issues often cause

the most conflicts on Enterprise Integration Patterns projects?

424. Eliminate unnecessary activities. Are there activities that came from a template or previous Enterprise Integration Patterns project that are not applicable on this phase of this Enterprise Integration Patterns project?

425. How can you address that situation?

426. How do you manage Enterprise Integration Patterns project Risk?

427. Did the Enterprise Integration Patterns project come in under budget?

428. How can slack be negative?

429. Meet requirements?

430. Your Enterprise Integration Patterns project management plan results in a Enterprise Integration Patterns project schedule that is too long. If the Enterprise Integration Patterns project network diagram cannot change and you have extra personnel resources, what is the BEST thing to do?

431. Did the final product meet or exceed user expectations?

2.20 Cost Management Plan: Enterprise Integration Patterns

432. Is it standard practice to formally commit stakeholders to the Enterprise Integration Patterns project via agreements?

433. Outside experts?

434. What weaknesses do you have?

435. Are corrective actions and variances reported?

436. Has the business need been clearly defined?

437. What is Enterprise Integration Patterns project cost management?

438. Is pert / critical path or equivalent methodology being used?

439. Are all vendor contracts closed out?

440. Are there checklists created to determine if all quality processes are followed?

441. Have process improvement efforts been completed before requirements efforts begin?

442. Who will prepare the cost estimates?

443. Personnel with expertise?

444. Who should write the PEP?

445. Have all documents been archived in a Enterprise Integration Patterns project repository for each release?

446. Have Enterprise Integration Patterns project management standards and procedures been identified / established and documented?

447. The definition of the Enterprise Integration Patterns project scope what needs to be accomplished?

448. Cost estimate preparation – What cost estimates will be prepared during the Enterprise Integration Patterns project phases?

449. Change types and category – What are the types of changes and what are the techniques to report and control changes?

450. Has the budget been baselined?

451. Are estimating assumptions and constraints captured?

2.21 Activity Cost Estimates: Enterprise Integration Patterns

452. Padding is bad and contingencies are good. what is the difference?

453. Specific - is the objective clear in terms of what, how, when, and where the situation will be changed?

454. What cost data should be used to estimate costs during the 2-year follow-up period?

455. Can you delete activities or make them inactive?

456. Who determines the quality and expertise of contractors?

457. How many activities should you have?

458. Is there anything unique in this Enterprise Integration Patterns projects scope statement that will affect resources?

459. Does the estimator have experience?

460. What are the audit requirements?

461. Why do you manage cost?

462. Are cost subtotals needed?

463. Does the activity rely on a common set of tools to carry it out?

464. Were you satisfied with the work?

465. Scope statement only direct or indirect costs as well?

466. What makes a good activity description?

467. How do you change activities?

468. What defines a successful Enterprise Integration Patterns project?

469. How quickly can the task be done with the skills available?

470. Does the estimator estimate by task or by person?

2.22 Cost Estimating Worksheet: Enterprise Integration Patterns

471. What will others want?

472. Does the Enterprise Integration Patterns project provide innovative ways for stakeholders to overcome obstacles or deliver better outcomes?

473. What costs are to be estimated?

474. What additional Enterprise Integration Patterns project(s) could be initiated as a result of this Enterprise Integration Patterns project?

475. Is it feasible to establish a control group arrangement?

476. What can be included?

477. How will the results be shared and to whom?

478. Ask: are others positioned to know, are others credible, and will others cooperate?

479. What is the estimated labor cost today based upon this information?

480. What happens to any remaining funds not used?

481. Who is best positioned to know and assist in identifying corresponding factors?

482. What is the purpose of estimating?

483. Is the Enterprise Integration Patterns project responsive to community need?

484. Identify the timeframe necessary to monitor progress and collect data to determine how the selected measure has changed?

485. Will the Enterprise Integration Patterns project collaborate with the local community and leverage resources?

486. Can a trend be established from historical performance data on the selected measure and are the criteria for using trend analysis or forecasting methods met?

2.23 Cost Baseline: Enterprise Integration Patterns

487. What is the consequence?

488. Are there contingencies or conditions related to the acceptance?

489. Is there anything you need from upper management in order to be successful?

490. If you sold 10x widgets on a day, what would the affect on profits be?

491. Does a process exist for establishing a cost baseline to measure Enterprise Integration Patterns project performance?

492. Has the documentation relating to operation and maintenance of the product(s) or service(s) been delivered to, and accepted by, operations management?

493. How likely is it to go wrong?

494. Does it impact schedule, cost, quality?

495. Has the appropriate access to relevant data and analysis capability been granted?

496. What is the most important thing to do next to make your Enterprise Integration Patterns project successful?

497. Is there anything unique in this Enterprise Integration Patterns projects scope statement that will affect resources?

498. Escalation criteria met?

499. Is the requested change request a result of changes in other Enterprise Integration Patterns project(s)?

500. When should cost estimates be developed?

501. Enterprise Integration Patterns project goals -should others be reconsidered?

502. How difficult will it be to do specific tasks on the Enterprise Integration Patterns project?

503. What deliverables come first?

504. What can go wrong?

2.24 Quality Management Plan: Enterprise Integration Patterns

505. Do you periodically review your data quality system to see that it is up to date and appropriate?

506. How does your organization maintain a safe and healthy work environment?

507. What field records are generated?

508. What are your organizations current levels and trends for the already stated measures related to employee wellbeing, satisfaction, and development?

509. Documented results available?

510. What are the established criteria that sampling / testing data are compared against?

511. Have adequate resources been provided by management to ensure Enterprise Integration Patterns project success?

512. How do you decide what information to record?

513. How long do you retain data?

514. Modifications to the requirements?

515. What type of in-house testing do you conduct?

516. How do you ensure that your sampling methods

and procedures meet your data needs?

517. How do you check in-coming sample material?

518. How does your organization recruit, hire, and retain new employees?

519. What is the audience for the data?

520. Have you eliminated all duplicative tasks or manual efforts, where appropriate?

521. Who needs a qmp?

522. Is the steering committee active in Enterprise Integration Patterns project oversight?

523. What are your key performance measures/indicators for tracking progress relative to your action plans?

2.25 Quality Metrics: Enterprise Integration Patterns

524. What is the benchmark?

525. Which are the right metrics to use?

526. What are your organizations next steps?

527. Are there any open risk issues?

528. Has risk analysis been adequately reviewed?

529. When will the Final Guidance will be issued?

530. Do the operators focus on determining; is there anything you need to worry about?

531. Is the reporting frequency appropriate?

532. What percentage are outcome-based?

533. Is a risk containment plan in place?

534. Is there alignment within your organization on definitions?

535. Are quality metrics defined?

536. Is quality culture a competitive advantage?

537. Which report did you use to create the data you are submitting?

538. How do you calculate such metrics?

539. What approved evidence based screening tools can be used?

540. Are interface issues coordinated?

541. How do you measure?

542. Have risk areas been identified?

543. What about still open problems?

2.26 Process Improvement Plan: Enterprise Integration Patterns

544. Has a process guide to collect the data been developed?

545. To elicit goal statements, do you ask a question such as, What do you want to achieve?

546. Why quality management?

547. What lessons have you learned so far?

548. The motive is determined by asking, Why do you want to achieve this goal?

549. Purpose of goal: the motive is determined by asking, why do you want to achieve this goal?

550. Where are you now?

551. Have the supporting tools been developed or acquired?

552. What actions are needed to address the problems and achieve the goals?

553. Management commitment at all levels?

554. Everyone agrees on what process improvement is, right?

555. Are you making progress on the improvement

framework?

556. What is the return on investment?

557. If a process improvement framework is being used, which elements will help the problems and goals listed?

558. Are there forms and procedures to collect and record the data?

559. Does your process ensure quality?

560. Modeling current processes is great, and will you ever see a return on that investment?

561. Have the frequency of collection and the points in the process where measurements will be made been determined?

562. What is the test-cycle concept?

2.27 Responsibility Assignment Matrix: Enterprise Integration Patterns

563. Does the contractors system provide unit or lot costs when applicable?

564. Do work packages consist of discrete tasks which are adequately described?

565. What do you need to implement earned value management?

566. Are work packages assigned to performing organizations?

567. Are material costs reported within the same period as that in which BCWP is earned for that material?

568. Are the requirements for all items of overhead established by rational, traceable processes?

569. Does the accounting system provide a basis for auditing records of direct costs chargeable to the contract?

570. The already stated responsible for the establishment of budgets and assignment of resources for overhead performance?

571. Budgeted cost for work scheduled?

572. Do all the identified groups or people really need to be consulted?

573. Does the contractors system identify work accomplishment against the schedule plan?

574. What travel needed?

575. Are people encouraged to bring up issues?

576. What do you do when people do not respond?

577. Cwbs elements to be subcontracted, with identification of subcontractors?

578. Will too many Communicating responsibilities tangle the Enterprise Integration Patterns project in unnecessary communications?

579. Do managers and team members provide helpful suggestions during review meetings?

580. Actual cost of work performed?

581. Are records maintained to show how management reserves are used?

582. Are the wbs and organizational levels for application of the Enterprise Integration Patterns projected overhead costs identified?

2.28 Roles and Responsibilities: Enterprise Integration Patterns

583. Accountabilities: what are the roles and responsibilities of individual team members?

584. What is working well?

585. Are the quality assurance functions and related roles and responsibilities clearly defined?

586. Are Enterprise Integration Patterns project team roles and responsibilities identified and documented?

587. Do the values and practices inherent in the culture of your organization foster or hinder the process?

588. What should you do now to ensure that you are meeting all expectations of your current position?

589. Be specific; avoid generalities. Thank you and great work alone are insufficient. What exactly do you appreciate and why?

590. Key conclusions and recommendations: Are conclusions and recommendations relevant and acceptable?

591. Was the expectation clearly communicated?

592. Required skills, knowledge, experience?

593. Is the data complete?

594. What should you do now to prepare for your career 5+ years from now?

595. Influence: what areas of organizational decision making are you able to influence when you do not have authority to make the final decision?

596. Is feedback clearly communicated and non-judgmental?

597. What areas of supervision are challenging for you?

598. What is working well within your organizations performance management system?

599. What specific behaviors did you observe?

600. What expectations were met?

601. Have you ever been a part of this team?

2.29 Human Resource Management Plan: Enterprise Integration Patterns

602. Are risk oriented checklists used during risk identification?

603. Who needs training?

604. Is an industry recognized support tool(s) being used for Enterprise Integration Patterns project scheduling & tracking?

605. Are procurement deliverables arriving on time and to specification?

606. Are post milestone Enterprise Integration Patterns project reviews (PMPR) conducted with your organization at least once a year?

607. Were decisions made in a timely manner?

608. Based on your Enterprise Integration Patterns project communication management plan, what worked well?

609. Are there dependencies with other initiatives or Enterprise Integration Patterns projects?

610. Have the key elements of a coherent Enterprise Integration Patterns project management strategy been established?

611. Are the quality tools and methods identified

in the Quality Plan appropriate to the Enterprise Integration Patterns project?

612. Who are the people that make up your organization and whom create the success that your organization enjoys as a whole?

613. Are Enterprise Integration Patterns project team members committed fulltime?

614. Are Enterprise Integration Patterns project contact logs kept up to date?

615. Pareto diagrams, statistical sampling, flow charting or trend analysis used quality monitoring?

616. Are risk triggers captured?

617. Identify who is needed on the core Enterprise Integration Patterns project team to complete Enterprise Integration Patterns project deliverables and achieve its goals and objectives. What skills, knowledge and experiences are required?

2.30 Communications Management Plan: Enterprise Integration Patterns

618. Who is responsible?

619. Who did you turn to if you had questions?

620. Are you constantly rushing from meeting to meeting?

621. Do you feel more overwhelmed by stakeholders?

622. Who will use or be affected by the result of a Enterprise Integration Patterns project?

623. Why do you manage communications?

624. What is the stakeholders level of authority?

625. Why is stakeholder engagement important?

626. Are stakeholders internal or external?

627. What help do you and your team need from the stakeholder?

628. Timing: when do the effects of the communication take place?

629. Which stakeholders are thought leaders, influences, or early adopters?

630. Who have you worked with in past, similar

initiatives?

631. Do you have members of your team responsible for certain stakeholders?

632. Which stakeholders can influence others?

633. Where do team members get information?

634. Do you then often overlook a key stakeholder or stakeholder group?

635. Are the stakeholders getting the information others need, are others consulted, are concerns addressed?

636. What to know?

2.31 Risk Management Plan: Enterprise Integration Patterns

637. Are the metrics meaningful and useful?

638. What will drive change?

639. Market risk -will the new service or product be useful to your organization or marketable to others?

640. Do you have a consistent repeatable process that is actually used?

641. What is the probability the risk avoidance strategy will be successful?

642. Should the risk be taken at all?

643. Are people attending meetings and doing work?

644. Why might it be late?

645. Is the customer willing to establish rapid communication links with the developer?

646. Where are you confronted with risks during the business phases?

647. Are enough people available?

648. How is the audit profession changing?

649. What does a risk management program do?

650. Do the people have the right combinations of skills?

651. Litigation – what is the probability that lawsuits will cause problems or delays in the Enterprise Integration Patterns project?

652. How risk averse are you?

653. How quickly does each item need to be resolved?

654. Are requirements fully understood by the software engineering team and customers?

655. Are you working on the right risks?

2.32 Risk Register: Enterprise Integration Patterns

656. Methodology: how will risk management be performed on this Enterprise Integration Patterns project?

657. Schedule impact/severity estimated range (workdays) assume the event happens, what is the potential impact?

658. What are the major risks facing the Enterprise Integration Patterns project?

659. Technology risk -is the Enterprise Integration Patterns project technically feasible?

660. Who is going to do it?

661. When would you develop a risk register?

662. What is the probability and impact of the risk occurring?

663. Manageability – have mitigations to the risk been identified?

664. Why would you develop a risk register?

665. Recovery actions - planned actions taken once a risk has occurred to allow you to move on. What should you do after?

666. User involvement: do you have the right users?

667. What has changed since the last period?

668. What are your key risks/show istoppers and what is being done to manage them?

669. People risk -are people with appropriate skills available to help complete the Enterprise Integration Patterns project?

670. Are there any gaps in the evidence?

671. When will it happen?

672. What could prevent you delivering on the strategic program objectives and what is being done to mitigate corresponding issues?

673. What is a Risk?

674. Preventative actions - planned actions to reduce the likelihood a risk will occur and/or reduce the seriousness should it occur. What should you do now?

2.33 Probability and Impact Assessment: Enterprise Integration Patterns

675. Are the risk data timely and relevant?

676. Are there any Enterprise Integration Patterns projects similar to this one in existence?

677. What action do you usually take against risks?

678. Who should be responsible for the monitoring and tracking of the indicators youhave identified?

679. Can the risk be avoided by choosing a different alternative?

680. When and how will the recent breakthroughs in basic research lead to commercial products?

681. Is a software Enterprise Integration Patterns project management tool available?

682. What is the Enterprise Integration Patterns project managers level of commitment and professionalism?

683. Can the Enterprise Integration Patterns project proceed without assuming the risk?

684. What is the past performance of the Enterprise Integration Patterns project manager?

685. Are testing tools available and suitable?

686. How well is the risk understood?

687. Do you train all developers in the process?

688. Have you worked with the customer in the past?

689. Are the risk data complete?

690. Supply/demand Enterprise Integration Patterns projections and trends; what are the levels of accuracy?

691. Is the number of people on the Enterprise Integration Patterns project team adequate to do the job?

692. Is the customer willing to commit significant time to the requirements gathering process?

693. Have customers been involved fully in the definition of requirements?

694. Is the Enterprise Integration Patterns project cutting across the entire organization?

2.34 Probability and Impact Matrix: Enterprise Integration Patterns

695. While preparing your risk responses, you identify additional risks. What should you do?

696. What are the methods to deal with risks?

697. What are data sources?

698. How well were you able to manage your risk?

699. Are team members trained in the use of the tools?

700. Which of the risk factors can be avoided altogether?

701. Mandated delivery date?

702. Costs associated with late delivery or a defective product?

703. Which should be probably done NEXT?

704. During Enterprise Integration Patterns project executing, a major problem occurs that was not included in the risk register. What should you do FIRST?

705. Do end-users have realistic expectations?

706. Do the requirements require the creation of new

algorithms?

707. How do risks change during the Enterprise Integration Patterns projects life cycle?

708. How completely has the customer been identified?

709. What has the Enterprise Integration Patterns project manager forgotten to do?

710. Are Enterprise Integration Patterns project requirements stable?

711. What is Enterprise Integration Patterns project risk management?

712. Risk may be made during which step of risk management?

2.35 Risk Data Sheet: Enterprise Integration Patterns

713. Do effective diagnostic tests exist?

714. Who has a vested interest in how you perform as your organization (our stakeholders)?

715. Has a sensitivity analysis been carried out?

716. What do people affected think about the need for, and practicality of preventive measures?

717. What are you here for (Mission)?

718. Are new hazards created?

719. What are you weak at and therefore need to do better?

720. Potential for recurrence?

721. How reliable is the data source?

722. What are you trying to achieve (Objectives)?

723. Risk of what?

724. How can hazards be reduced?

725. What can you do?

726. What is the likelihood of it happening?

727. Type of risk identified?

728. During work activities could hazards exist?

729. What will be the consequences if it happens?

730. What are the main opportunities available to you that you should grab while you can?

731. Will revised controls lead to tolerable risk levels?

2.36 Procurement Management Plan: Enterprise Integration Patterns

732. Has your organization readiness assessment been conducted?

733. Has the scope management document been updated and distributed to help prevent scope creep?

734. Are assumptions being identified, recorded, analyzed, qualified and closed?

735. Is there an on-going process in place to monitor Enterprise Integration Patterns project risks?

736. Have Enterprise Integration Patterns project team accountabilities & responsibilities been clearly defined?

737. How will you coordinate Procurement with aspects of the Enterprise Integration Patterns project?

738. Is there an issues management plan in place?

739. Sensitivity analysis?

740. Are the budget estimates reasonable?

741. How long will it take for the purchase cost to be the same as the lease cost?

742. How and when do you enter into Enterprise Integration Patterns project Procurement

Management?

743. Public engagement – did you get it right?

744. Was the scope definition used in task sequencing?

745. Does the business case include how the Enterprise Integration Patterns project aligns with your organizations strategic goals & objectives?

746. Are the key elements of a Enterprise Integration Patterns project Charter present?

747. Are the quality tools and methods identified in the Quality Plan appropriate to the Enterprise Integration Patterns project?

748. Is the Enterprise Integration Patterns project sponsor clearly communicating the business case or rationale for why this Enterprise Integration Patterns project is needed?

749. What are your quality assurance overheads?

2.37 Source Selection Criteria: Enterprise Integration Patterns

750. How do you facilitate evaluation against published criteria?

751. Do you want to have them collaborate at subfactor level?

752. How should the oral presentations be handled?

753. How much weight should be placed on past performance information?

754. Are there any common areas of weaknesses or deficiencies in the proposals in the competitive range?

755. What does an evaluation address and what does a sample resemble?

756. Are resultant proposal revisions allowed?

757. What is the basis of an estimate and what assumptions were made?

758. What is cost analysis and when should it be performed?

759. Will the technical evaluation factor unnecessarily force the acquisition into a higher-priced market segment?

760. What should preproposal conferences accomplish?

761. How should comments received in response to a RFP be handled?

762. What is the role of counsel in the procurement process?

763. Is the contracting office likely to receive more purchase requests for this item or service during the coming year?

764. What does a sample rating scale look like?

765. What is the last item a Enterprise Integration Patterns project manager must do to finalize Enterprise Integration Patterns project close-out?

766. What documentation is needed for a tradeoff decision?

767. What should be the contracting officers strategy?

768. What documentation should be used to support the selection decision?

2.38 Stakeholder Management Plan: Enterprise Integration Patterns

769. What sources of information are reliable?

770. Does the Enterprise Integration Patterns project have a Quality Culture?

771. Does the Enterprise Integration Patterns project have a Statement of Work?

772. Is the Enterprise Integration Patterns project sponsor clearly communicating the business case or rationale for why this Enterprise Integration Patterns project is needed?

773. Who will be responsible for managing and maintaining the Issues Register?

774. What is the general purpose in defining responsibilities of the already stated affiliated with the Enterprise Integration Patterns project?

775. Are the Enterprise Integration Patterns project plans updated on a frequent basis?

776. Are updated Enterprise Integration Patterns project time & resource estimates reasonable based on the current Enterprise Integration Patterns project stage?

777. How are the overall Enterprise Integration Patterns project development processes to be

undertaken to produce the Enterprise Integration Patterns project outputs?

778. Can the requirements be traced to the appropriate components of the solution, as well as test scripts?

779. Is the amount of effort justified by the anticipated value of forming a new process?

780. How will the equipment be verified?

781. What action will be taken once reports have been received?

782. Which impacts could serve as impediments?

783. Has the schedule been baselined?

784. Are vendor invoices audited for accuracy before payment?

785. Are the payment terms being followed?

786. Does this include subcontracted development?

2.39 Change Management Plan: Enterprise Integration Patterns

787. What will be the preferred method of delivery?

788. What does a resilient organization look like?

789. What are the dependencies?

790. Where do you want to be?

791. Who might present the most resistance?

792. Where will the funds come from?

793. How badly can information be misinterpreted?

794. How much Enterprise Integration Patterns project management is needed?

795. Who is the target audience of the piece of information?

796. Do you need new systems?

797. How does the principle of senders and receivers make the Enterprise Integration Patterns project communications effort more complex?

798. What is going to be done differently?

799. Will the culture embrace or reject this change?

800. What can you do to minimise misinterpretation and negative perceptions?

801. Do you need a new organization structure?

802. What relationships will change?

803. What are the training strategies?

804. What type of materials/channels will be available to leverage?

805. Will all field readiness criteria have been practically met prior to training roll-out?

3.0 Executing Process Group: Enterprise Integration Patterns

806. What is involved in the solicitation process?

807. How can software assist in procuring goods and services?

808. How do you control progress of your Enterprise Integration Patterns project?

809. Will outside resources be needed to help?

810. Were sponsors and decision makers available when needed outside regularly scheduled meetings?

811. What are the key components of the Enterprise Integration Patterns project communications plan?

812. What areas were overlooked on this Enterprise Integration Patterns project?

813. Are decisions made in a timely manner?

814. In what way has the program come up with innovative measures for problem-solving?

815. Would you rate yourself as being risk-averse, risk-neutral, or risk-seeking?

816. How does the job market and current state of the economy affect human resource management?

817. How could stakeholders negatively impact your Enterprise Integration Patterns project?

818. How well defined and documented were the Enterprise Integration Patterns project management processes you chose to use?

819. What are some crucial elements of a good Enterprise Integration Patterns project plan?

820. When will the Enterprise Integration Patterns project be done?

821. What are the critical steps involved with strategy mapping?

822. What are the critical steps involved in selecting measures and initiatives?

823. How will professionals learn what is expected from them what the deliverables are?

3.1 Team Member Status Report: Enterprise Integration Patterns

824. Are your organizations Enterprise Integration Patterns projects more successful over time?

825. How it is to be done?

826. How does this product, good, or service meet the needs of the Enterprise Integration Patterns project and your organization as a whole?

827. Do you have an Enterprise Enterprise Integration Patterns project Management Office (EPMO)?

828. Why is it to be done?

829. Does the product, good, or service already exist within your organization?

830. Will the staff do training or is that done by a third party?

831. How much risk is involved?

832. When a teams productivity and success depend on collaboration and the efficient flow of information, what generally fails them?

833. Does every department have to have a Enterprise Integration Patterns project Manager on staff?

834. Does your organization have the means (staff,

money, contract, etc.) to produce or to acquire the product, good, or service?

835. What specific interest groups do you have in place?

836. How can you make it practical?

837. What is to be done?

838. How will resource planning be done?

839. Is there evidence that staff is taking a more professional approach toward management of your organizations Enterprise Integration Patterns projects?

840. Are the attitudes of staff regarding Enterprise Integration Patterns project work improving?

841. The problem with Reward & Recognition Programs is that the truly deserving people all too often get left out. How can you make it practical?

842. Are the products of your organizations Enterprise Integration Patterns projects meeting customers objectives?

3.2 Change Request: Enterprise Integration Patterns

843. Who can suggest changes?

844. Why do you want to have a change control system?

845. What is the relationship between requirements attributes and reliability?

846. Will there be a change request form in use?

847. Who is communicating the change?

848. Are there requirements attributes that can discriminate between high and low reliability?

849. What are the requirements for urgent changes?

850. How is quality being addressed on the Enterprise Integration Patterns project?

851. How does your organization control changes before and after software is released to a customer?

852. What is the function of the change control committee?

853. Who needs to approve change requests?

854. Where do changes come from?

855. Has a formal technical review been conducted to assess technical correctness?

856. What are the basic mechanics of the Change Advisory Board (CAB)?

857. Have all related configuration items been properly updated?

858. Who is responsible to authorize changes?

859. What mechanism is used to appraise others of changes that are made?

860. How are the measures for carrying out the change established?

3.3 Change Log: Enterprise Integration Patterns

861. Do the described changes impact on the integrity or security of the system?

862. Does the suggested change request seem to represent a necessary enhancement to the product?

863. When was the request approved?

864. Is this a mandatory replacement?

865. How does this relate to the standards developed for specific business processes?

866. Is the change request within Enterprise Integration Patterns project scope?

867. Is the change backward compatible without limitations?

868. Will the Enterprise Integration Patterns project fail if the change request is not executed?

869. Is the submitted change a new change or a modification of a previously approved change?

870. Who initiated the change request?

871. How does this change affect scope?

872. How does this change affect the timeline of the

schedule?

873. Does the suggested change request represent a desired enhancement to the products functionality?

874. When was the request submitted?

875. Should a more thorough impact analysis be conducted?

876. Is the requested change request a result of changes in other Enterprise Integration Patterns project(s)?

877. Is the change request open, closed or pending?

3.4 Decision Log: Enterprise Integration Patterns

878. Which variables make a critical difference?

879. How does the use a Decision Support System influence the strategies/tactics or costs?

880. What eDiscovery problem or issue did your organization set out to fix or make better?

881. Linked to original objective?

882. Who is the decisionmaker?

883. How effective is maintaining the log at facilitating organizational learning?

884. Is everything working as expected?

885. What is your overall strategy for quality control / quality assurance procedures?

886. How do you know when you are achieving it?

887. Who will be given a copy of this document and where will it be kept?

888. Decision-making process; how will the team make decisions?

889. How consolidated and comprehensive a story can you tell by capturing currently available incident

data in a central location and through a log of key decisions during an incident?

890. Meeting purpose; why does this team meet?

891. What was the rationale for the decision?

892. How do you define success?

893. How does provision of information, both in terms of content and presentation, influence acceptance of alternative strategies?

894. Adversarial environment. is your opponent open to a non-traditional workflow, or will it likely challenge anything you do?

895. What makes you different or better than others companies selling the same thing?

896. What are the cost implications?

897. At what point in time does loss become unacceptable?

3.5 Quality Audit: Enterprise Integration Patterns

898. What experience do staff have in the type of work that the audit entails?

899. Has a written procedure been established to identify devices during all stages of receipt, reconditioning, distribution and installation so that mix-ups are prevented?

900. How does your organization know that it is effectively and constructively guiding staff through to timely completion of tasks?

901. Is your organizational structure a help or a hindrance to deployment?

902. Are all employees made aware of device defects which may occur from the improper performance of specific jobs?

903. Is your organizational structure established and each positions responsibility defined?

904. Is progress against the intentions measurable?

905. How does your organization know that its staff placements are appropriately effective and constructive in relation to program-related learning outcomes?

906. How does your organization know that its risk

management system is appropriately effective and constructive?

907. Are training programs documented?

908. How does your organization know that its staff are presenting original work, and properly acknowledging the work of others?

909. How are you auditing your organizations compliance with regulations?

910. What does an analysis of your organizations staff profile suggest in terms of its planning, and how is this being addressed?

911. How does your organization know that the system for managing its facilities is appropriately effective and constructive?

912. How does your organization know that its Mission, Vision and Values Statements are appropriate and effectively guiding your organization?

913. Are all staff empowered and encouraged to contribute to ongoing improvement efforts?

914. How do you indicate the extent to which your personnel would be expected to contribute to the work effort?

915. How does your organization know whether they are adhering to mission and achieving objectives?

916. How does your organization know that its relationship with its (past) staff is appropriately

effective and constructive?

917. Are all records associated with the reconditioning of a device maintained for a minimum of two years after the sale or disposal of the last device within a lot of merchandise?

3.6 Team Directory: Enterprise Integration Patterns

918. Process decisions: are all start-up, turn over and close out requirements of the contract satisfied?

919. Who will write the meeting minutes and distribute?

920. Contract requirements complied with?

921. What needs to be communicated?

922. Process decisions: how well was task order work performed?

923. Decisions: is the most suitable form of contract being used?

924. Is construction on schedule?

925. How does the team resolve conflicts and ensure tasks are completed?

926. Process decisions: are there any statutory or regulatory issues relevant to the timely execution of work?

927. Who will be the stakeholders on your next Enterprise Integration Patterns project?

928. Who are the Team Members?

929. Where will the product be used and/or delivered or built when appropriate?

930. Decisions: what could be done better to improve the quality of the constructed product?

931. Who will talk to the customer?

932. How will you accomplish and manage the objectives?

933. Process decisions: which organizational elements and which individuals will be assigned management functions?

934. Process decisions: do job conditions warrant additional actions to collect job information and document on-site activity?

935. How will the team handle changes?

936. Days from the time the issue is identified?

3.7 Team Operating Agreement: Enterprise Integration Patterns

937. Do you upload presentation materials in advance and test the technology?

938. Do you ensure that all participants know how to use the required technology?

939. Did you draft the meeting agenda?

940. Resource allocation: how will individual team members account for time and expenses, and how will this be allocated in the team budget?

941. What is culture?

942. How does teaming fit in with overall organizational goals and meet organizational needs?

943. Are there the right people on your team?

944. What individual strengths does each team member bring to the group?

945. Do you vary your voice pace, tone and pitch to engage participants and gain involvement?

946. What is your unique contribution to your organization?

947. Do you prevent individuals from dominating the meeting?

948. Are there more than two functional areas represented by your team?

949. Did you prepare participants for the next meeting?

950. To whom do you deliver your services?

951. What is a Virtual Team?

952. What resources can be provided for the team in terms of equipment, space, time for training, protected time and space for meetings, and travel allowances?

953. Do you leverage technology engagement tools group chat, polls, screen sharing, etc.?

954. Are leadership responsibilities shared among team members (versus a single leader)?

955. What are the current caseload numbers in the unit?

3.8 Team Performance Assessment: Enterprise Integration Patterns

956. To what degree does the teams work approach provide opportunity for members to engage in fact-based problem solving?

957. Can familiarity breed backup?

958. When does the medium matter?

959. To what degree will new and supplemental skills be introduced as the need is recognized?

960. To what degree does the teams approach to its work allow for modification and improvement over time?

961. What are you doing specifically to develop the leaders around you?

962. To what degree do team members frequently explore the teams purpose and its implications?

963. To what degree are the skill areas critical to team performance present?

964. To what degree can team members frequently and easily communicate with one another?

965. To what degree do the goals specify concrete team work products?

966. If you have criticized someones work for method variance in your role as reviewer, what was the circumstance?

967. What makes opportunities more or less obvious?

968. What do you think is the most constructive thing that could be done now to resolve considerations and disputes about method variance?

969. Do you give group members authority to make at least some important decisions?

970. To what degree are sub-teams possible or necessary?

971. To what degree will the team ensure that all members equitably share the work essential to the success of the team?

972. To what degree does the team possess adequate membership to achieve its ends?

973. How hard do you try to make a good selection?

974. To what degree are staff involved as partners in the improvement process?

3.9 Team Member Performance Assessment: Enterprise Integration Patterns

975. For what period of time is a member rated?

976. What are best practices for delivering and developing training evaluations to maximize the benefits of leveraging emerging technologies?

977. Goals met?

978. To what degree are the teams goals and objectives clear, simple, and measurable?

979. How do you currently account for your results in the teams achievement?

980. What makes them effective?

981. How often are assessments to be conducted?

982. To what degree can team members meet frequently enough to accomplish the teams ends?

983. To what degree do members articulate the goals beyond the team membership?

984. Are there any safeguards to prevent intentional or unintentional rating errors?

985. How do you use data to inform instruction and improve staff achievement?

986. To what degree are the goals realistic?

987. Is it clear how goals will be accomplished?

988. Does adaptive training work?

989. How was the determination made for which training platforms would be used (i.e., media selection)?

990. How often should assessments be conducted?

991. What happens if a team member receives a Rating of Unsatisfactory?

992. Why do performance reviews?

3.10 Issue Log: Enterprise Integration Patterns

993. What approaches do you use?

994. In classifying stakeholders, which approach to do so are you using?

995. What help do you and your team need from the stakeholders?

996. What is the status of the issue?

997. Is access to the Issue Log controlled?

998. What approaches to you feel are the best ones to use?

999. What does the stakeholder need from the team?

1000. What is a change?

1001. Are they needed?

1002. How do you manage communications?

1003. Do you prepare stakeholder engagement plans?

1004. Who needs to know and how much?

1005. How do you manage human resources?

1006. Is there an important stakeholder who is

actively opposed and will not receive messages?

1007. Who reported the issue?

1008. Do you feel a register helps?

4.0 Monitoring and Controlling Process Group: Enterprise Integration Patterns

1009. Just how important is your work to the overall success of the Enterprise Integration Patterns project?

1010. Purpose: toward what end is the evaluation being conducted?

1011. Use: how will they use the information?

1012. Is there undesirable impact on staff or resources?

1013. What factors are contributing to progress or delay in the achievement of products and results?

1014. What resources are necessary?

1015. Change, where should you look for problems?

1016. What is the timeline for the Enterprise Integration Patterns project?

1017. Feasibility: how much money, time, and effort can you put into this?

1018. How is agile program management done?

1019. Are there areas that need improvement?

1020. User: who wants the information and what are

they interested in?

1021. Is there sufficient funding available for this?

1022. How well defined and documented were the Enterprise Integration Patterns project management processes you chose to use?

1023. How is agile portfolio management done?

1024. If a risk event occurs, what will you do?

1025. Is the program making progress in helping to achieve the set results?

1026. Is there adequate validation on required fields?

4.1 Project Performance Report: Enterprise Integration Patterns

1027. To what degree are the demands of the task compatible with and converge with the relationships of the informal organization?

1028. To what degree are the structures of the formal organization consistent with the behaviors in the informal organization?

1029. To what degree does the informal organization make use of individual resources and meet individual needs?

1030. To what degree do the relationships of the informal organization motivate taskrelevant behavior and facilitate task completion?

1031. What is the degree to which rules govern information exchange between groups?

1032. How can Enterprise Integration Patterns project sustainability be maintained?

1033. What is the degree to which rules govern information exchange between individuals within your organization?

1034. To what degree can the team measure progress against specific goals?

1035. To what degree will the approach capitalize

on and enhance the skills of all team members in a manner that takes into consideration other demands on members of the team?

1036. How is the data used?

1037. To what degree are the members clear on what they are individually responsible for and what they are jointly responsible for?

1038. To what degree do team members agree with the goals, relative importance, and the ways in which achievement will be measured?

1039. To what degree does the teams work approach provide opportunity for members to engage in results-based evaluation?

4.2 Variance Analysis: Enterprise Integration Patterns

1040. What types of services and expense are shared between business segments?

1041. Are indirect costs accumulated for comparison with the corresponding budgets?

1042. What is the performance to date and material commitment?

1043. Does the scheduling system identify in a timely manner the status of work?

1044. Are your organizations and items of cost assigned to each pool identified?

1045. What should management do?

1046. Other relevant issues of Variance Analysis -selling price or gross margin?

1047. Did an existing competitor change strategy?

1048. Favorable or unfavorable variance?

1049. What business event caused the fluctuation?

1050. What are the actual costs to date?

1051. At what point should variances be isolated and brought to the attention of the management?

1052. What is the total budget for the Enterprise Integration Patterns project (including estimates for authorized and unpriced work)?

1053. What is the incurrence of actual indirect costs in excess of budgets, by element of expense?

1054. Are authorized changes being incorporated in a timely manner?

1055. How do you identify potential or actual overruns and underruns?

1056. What is the dollar amount of the fluctuation?

1057. When, during the last four quarters, did a primary business event occur causing a fluctuation?

1058. Are all cwbs elements specified for external reporting?

1059. Why are standard cost systems used?

4.3 Earned Value Status: Enterprise Integration Patterns

1060. Are you hitting your Enterprise Integration Patterns projects targets?

1061. How does this compare with other Enterprise Integration Patterns projects?

1062. How much is it going to cost by the finish?

1063. Verification is a process of ensuring that the developed system satisfies the stakeholders agreements and specifications; Are you building the product right? What do you verify?

1064. What is the unit of forecast value?

1065. Where are your problem areas?

1066. Where is evidence-based earned value in your organization reported?

1067. If earned value management (EVM) is so good in determining the true status of a Enterprise Integration Patterns project and Enterprise Integration Patterns project its completion, why is it that hardly any one uses it in information systems related Enterprise Integration Patterns projects?

1068. Earned value can be used in almost any Enterprise Integration Patterns project situation and in almost any Enterprise Integration Patterns project environment. it may be used on large Enterprise Integration Patterns projects, medium sized Enterprise Integration Patterns projects, tiny Enterprise Integration Patterns projects (in cut-down form), complex and simple Enterprise Integration Patterns projects and in any market sector. some people, of course, know all about earned value, they have used it for years - but perhaps not as effectively as they could have?

1069. When is it going to finish?

1070. Validation is a process of ensuring that the developed system will actually achieve the stakeholders desired outcomes; Are you building the right product? What do you validate?

4.4 Risk Audit: Enterprise Integration Patterns

1071. Why do audits fail?

1072. Do you manage the process through use of metrics?

1073. What is the Board doing to assure measurement and improve outcomes and quality and reduce avoidable adverse events?

1074. Are some people working on multiple Enterprise Integration Patterns projects?

1075. Do requirements put excessive performance constraints on the product?

1076. Is risk an management agenda item?

1077. Does the adoption of a business risk audit approach change internal control documentation and testing practices?

1078. How can the strategy fail/achieved?

1079. Who is responsible for what?

1080. Can analytical tests provide evidence that is as strong as evidence from traditional substantive tests?

1081. Are tool mentors available?

1082. To what extent are auditors effective at linking business risks and management assertions?

1083. What impact does experience with one client have on decisions made for other clients during the risk-assessment process?

1084. What events or circumstances could affect the achievement of your objectives?

1085. What is the anticipated volatility of the requirements?

1086. Does your organization have a register of insurance policies detailing all current insurance policies?

1087. Are Enterprise Integration Patterns project requirements stable?

1088. If applicable; which route/packaging option do you choose for transport of hazmat material?

1089. How effective are your risk controls?

4.5 Contractor Status Report: Enterprise Integration Patterns

1090. Who can list a Enterprise Integration Patterns project as organization experience, your organization or a previous employee of your organization?

1091. What was the budget or estimated cost for your organizations services?

1092. What was the final actual cost?

1093. Describe how often regular updates are made to the proposed solution. Are corresponding regular updates included in the standard maintenance plan?

1094. What was the actual budget or estimated cost for your organizations services?

1095. What was the overall budget or estimated cost?

1096. What are the minimum and optimal bandwidth requirements for the proposed solution?

1097. How is risk transferred?

1098. How long have you been using the services?

1099. If applicable; describe your standard schedule for new software version releases. Are new software version releases included in the standard maintenance plan?

1100. What is the average response time for answering a support call?

1101. How does the proposed individual meet each requirement?

1102. What process manages the contracts?

1103. Are there contractual transfer concerns?

4.6 Formal Acceptance: Enterprise Integration Patterns

1104. What was done right?

1105. Was the Enterprise Integration Patterns project managed well?

1106. How does your team plan to obtain formal acceptance on your Enterprise Integration Patterns project?

1107. Have all comments been addressed?

1108. Was the client satisfied with the Enterprise Integration Patterns project results?

1109. Is formal acceptance of the Enterprise Integration Patterns project product documented and distributed?

1110. Do you buy-in installation services?

1111. Does it do what client said it would?

1112. Do you perform formal acceptance or burn-in tests?

1113. What lessons were learned about your Enterprise Integration Patterns project management methodology?

1114. How well did the team follow the methodology?

1115. General estimate of the costs and times to complete the Enterprise Integration Patterns project?

1116. Did the Enterprise Integration Patterns project achieve its MOV?

1117. Was the Enterprise Integration Patterns project goal achieved?

1118. Who would use it?

1119. Who supplies data?

1120. Was the Enterprise Integration Patterns project work done on time, within budget, and according to specification?

1121. Was the sponsor/customer satisfied?

1122. Was business value realized?

1123. What features, practices, and processes proved to be strengths or weaknesses?

5.0 Closing Process Group: Enterprise Integration Patterns

1124. If action is called for, what form should it take?

1125. How well did the team follow the chosen processes?

1126. Did the Enterprise Integration Patterns project team have enough people to execute the Enterprise Integration Patterns project plan?

1127. Did you do things well?

1128. Was the user/client satisfied with the end product?

1129. What is the risk of failure to your organization?

1130. How will you do it?

1131. Is there a clear cause and effect between the activity and the lesson learned?

1132. What was learned?

1133. Contingency planning. if a risk event occurs, what will you do?

1134. What is the overall risk of the Enterprise Integration Patterns project to your organization?

1135. Just how important is your work to the overall

success of the Enterprise Integration Patterns project?

1136. Is this a follow-on to a previous Enterprise Integration Patterns project?

1137. What could be done to improve the process?

1138. Were cost budgets met?

1139. How will staff learn how to use the deliverables?

1140. Were escalated issues resolved promptly?

5.1 Procurement Audit: Enterprise Integration Patterns

1141. Was the outcome of the award process properly reached and communicated?

1142. Did the conditions included in the contract protect the risk of non-performance by the supplier and were there no conflicting provisions?

1143. Was the suitability of candidates accurately assessed?

1144. Is there no evidence that the expert has influenced the decisions taken by the public authority in his/her interest or in the interest of a specific contractor?

1145. Does each policy statement contain the legal reference(s) on which the policy is based?

1146. Can small orders such as magazine subscriptions and non-product items such as membership in organizations be processed by the ordering department?

1147. Could bidders learn all relevant information straight from the tender documents?

1148. Is the relationship between in-house and external work considered in the strategy?

1149. Are the pages of the minutes book press prenumbered?

1150. Did the chosen procedure ensure fair competition and transparency?

1151. Proper and complete records of transactions and events are maintained?

1152. Is there a practice that prohibits signing blank purchase orders?

1153. Did the bidder comply with requests within the deadline set?

1154. Have guidelines been set up for how the procurement process should be conducted?

1155. Does the procurement function/unit have the ability to negotiate with customers and suppliers?

1156. Is there a procedure on requesting bids?

1157. Were no charges billed to interested economic operators or the parties to the system?

1158. Are outsourcing and Public Private Partnerships considered as alternatives to in-house work?

1159. Are review meetings organized during contract execution and do they meet demand?

1160. Was suitability of candidates accurately assessed?

5.2 Contract Close-Out: Enterprise Integration Patterns

1161. How/when used ?

1162. Has each contract been audited to verify acceptance and delivery?

1163. Parties: who is involved?

1164. Was the contract complete without requiring numerous changes and revisions?

1165. How does it work?

1166. How is the contracting office notified of the automatic contract close-out?

1167. Change in knowledge?

1168. Parties: Authorized?

1169. Was the contract sufficiently clear so as not to result in numerous disputes and misunderstandings?

1170. Have all acceptance criteria been met prior to final payment to contractors?

1171. What happens to the recipient of services?

1172. Why Outsource?

1173. What is capture management?

1174. Change in circumstances?

1175. Change in attitude or behavior?

1176. Have all contract records been included in the Enterprise Integration Patterns project archives?

1177. Are the signers the authorized officials?

1178. Have all contracts been completed?

1179. Have all contracts been closed?

1180. Was the contract type appropriate?

5.3 Project or Phase Close-Out: Enterprise Integration Patterns

1181. Were risks identified and mitigated?

1182. What security considerations needed to be addressed during the procurement life cycle?

1183. If you were the Enterprise Integration Patterns project sponsor, how would you determine which Enterprise Integration Patterns project team(s) and/or individuals deserve recognition?

1184. What hierarchical authority does the stakeholder have in your organization?

1185. How much influence did the stakeholder have over others?

1186. What information did each stakeholder need to contribute to the Enterprise Integration Patterns projects success?

1187. In preparing the Lessons Learned report, should it reflect a consensus viewpoint, or should the report reflect the different individual viewpoints?

1188. What are the informational communication needs for each stakeholder?

1189. Is the lesson based on actual Enterprise Integration Patterns project experience rather than on independent research?

1190. What are the mandatory communication needs for each stakeholder?

1191. When and how were information needs best met?

1192. Did the delivered product meet the specified requirements and goals of the Enterprise Integration Patterns project?

1193. Who controlled key decisions that were made?

1194. Which changes might a stakeholder be required to make as a result of the Enterprise Integration Patterns project?

1195. What information is each stakeholder group interested in?

1196. Is the lesson significant, valid, and applicable?

1197. Were messages directly related to the release strategy or phases of the Enterprise Integration Patterns project?

5.4 Lessons Learned: Enterprise Integration Patterns

1198. Who has execution authority?

1199. Are you in full regulatory compliance?

1200. How did the estimated Enterprise Integration Patterns project Budget compare with the total actual expenditures?

1201. How was the quality of products/processes assured?

1202. What is the supplier dependency?

1203. Was Enterprise Integration Patterns project performance validated or challenged?

1204. What is your working hypothesis, if you have one?

1205. How timely was the training you received in preparation for the use of the product/service?

1206. What did you put in place to ensure success?

1207. How well does the product or service the Enterprise Integration Patterns project produced meet your needs?

1208. What rewards do the individuals seek?

1209. How effective were your design reviews?

1210. Overall, how effective were the efforts to prepare you and your organization for the impact of the product/service of the Enterprise Integration Patterns project?

1211. What skills did you need that were missing on this Enterprise Integration Patterns project?

1212. Were any objectives unmet?

1213. How satisfied are you with your involvement in the development and/or review of the Enterprise Integration Patterns project Scope during Enterprise Integration Patterns project Initiation and Planning?

1214. If issue escalation was required, how effectively were issues resolved?

1215. Was sufficient advance training conducted and/or information provided to enable the already stated affected by the changes to adjust to and accommodate them?

1216. How efficient and effective were meetings?

Index

ability 35, 132, 267
acceptable 106, 111, 203
acceptance 9, 49, 152-153, 193, 236, 262, 268
accepted 193
accepting 150
access 4, 10-12, 51, 59-61, 96, 100, 129, 193, 248
accessed 105
accomplish 10, 87, 171, 222, 241, 246
accordance 185
according 35, 39, 263
account 30, 242, 246
accounted 45
accounting 201
accrue 150
accuracy 45, 51, 101, 159, 214, 224
accurate 12, 155, 167, 181, 185
accurately 266-267
achieve 10, 54, 172, 199, 206, 217, 245, 251, 257, 263
achieved 24, 47, 258, 263
achieving 107, 235, 238
acquire 230
acquired 169, 199
across 111, 133, 149, 214
action 125, 150, 160, 164-165, 196, 213, 224, 264
actions 80, 144, 164, 187, 199, 211-212, 241
active 196
actively 249
activities 53, 63, 78, 153, 168-172, 174-176, 178, 183-186, 189-190, 218
activity 5-6, 30, 32, 129, 146, 168-169, 171-173, 175, 177, 180, 183, 189-190, 241, 264
actual 30, 164, 202, 254-255, 260, 270, 272
actually 35, 136, 167, 209, 257
adaptive 247
adding 77, 82, 89
additional 33, 54, 103, 129, 191, 215, 241
additions 83
address 1, 20, 68, 72, 115, 186, 199, 221
addressed 95, 148, 177, 208, 231, 238, 262, 270
addressing 35

adequate		86, 165, 195, 214, 245, 251
adequately	33, 56, 197, 201
adhered		164
adhering		238
adjust 273
adopted		103
adopters		137, 207
adopting		89
adoption		129, 131, 136, 258
advance		242, 273
advantage	1, 197
advantages	57, 89, 174
adverse		258
advise 2
Advisory		232
affect 26, 90, 97, 110, 144, 156, 158, 189, 193-194, 227, 233, 259
affected		53, 207, 217, 273
affecting		14
affects 180
affiliated		223
affordable	68
against 39, 44, 195, 202, 213, 221, 237, 252
agenda		242, 258
aggregate	130
aggregated	59
agility 100
agreed		41, 43
Agreement	8, 44, 152, 242
agreements	151, 187, 256
agrees 199
algorithms	216
aligned		20, 62
alignment	151, 197
aligns 220
alleged		3
allocate		112, 119
allocated		132, 242
allocating	165
allocation	165, 242
allowances	243
allowed		2, 221
allows 12
almost 256

275

already   98, 137, 195, 201, 223, 229, 273
alternate   121
altogether   215
always 12
amount   25, 64, 99, 106, 224, 255
amounts   61
analysis   4, 8, 12-13, 47, 68-70, 144, 192-193, 197, 206, 217, 219, 221, 234, 238, 254
analysts   46
analytical   46, 258
analytics   46
analyze   4, 45, 49, 71
analyzed   70, 219
annual 164
another   54, 87, 94-95, 104, 115, 117, 162, 180, 244
answer 13-14, 18, 29, 41, 49, 65, 76, 85
answered   27, 40, 48, 64, 75, 84, 137
answering   13, 261
anybody   146
anyone   37, 150
anything   119, 148, 168, 177, 189, 193-194, 197, 236
appear   3
appears   79
applicable   13, 153, 186, 201, 259-260, 271
applied   171, 181
appointed   34-35
appraise   232
appreciate   203
approach   66, 109, 112, 114, 124, 132, 230, 244, 248, 252-253, 258
approaches   87, 105, 123, 248
approval   54
approvals   153, 161
approve   159, 231
approved   26, 67, 156, 198, 233
approving   156
Architects   10
archived   188
archives   269
arising 139
around 244
arrive 50
arrives 88

arriving 205
articulate		246
ascertain		165
asking 3, 10, 199
aspects		219
assertions		259
assess 176, 232
assessable		180
assessed		266-267
Assessment		7-8, 11-12, 21, 213, 219, 244, 246
assets 92
assigned		30, 36, 110, 123, 142, 162, 164, 168, 171, 201, 241, 254
assigning		179
Assignment		6, 201
assist 11, 50, 73, 181, 191, 227
assistant		10
associate		99, 133
associated		91, 155, 215, 239
assume		211
assuming		213
Assumption		5, 160
assurance		203, 220, 235
assure 45, 258
assured		51, 272
attainable		38
attempt		106, 127
attempted		37
attempts		97, 107, 121, 123
attendance		35
attendant		71
attended		1, 35
attending		209
attention		14, 254
attitude		108, 269
attitudes		230
attractive		97
attribute		161
attributes		5, 155, 171, 231
audience		196, 225
audited		224, 268
auditing		81, 161, 201, 238
auditors		259

audits 258
author 3
authority   152-153, 165, 204, 207, 245, 266, 270, 272
authorize   232
authorized   148, 165, 255, 268-269
automate   55
automated   60, 150
automatic   268
automation   132
autonomy   96
available   18, 31, 33, 38, 79, 98, 100, 103, 108, 124, 130, 134, 139, 149, 164, 169, 175, 185, 190, 195, 209, 212-214, 218, 226-227, 235, 251, 258
Average   14, 28, 40, 48, 64, 75, 84, 115, 137, 261
averse 210
avoidable   258
avoidance   209
avoided   213, 215
awareness   144
backend   53
background   12
backup   244
backward   233
balance   44, 112
balanced   106
bandwidth   260
barrier 136
barriers 90, 105, 124
Baseline   6, 47, 152, 193
baselined   45, 188, 224
because   2, 185
become   133, 156, 236
before 1-2, 12, 37, 121, 141, 175, 183, 187, 224, 231
beginning   4, 17, 28, 40, 48, 64, 75, 84, 137
behavior   42, 252, 269
behaviors   23, 144, 204, 252
behind 2
belief   13, 18, 29, 41, 49, 65, 76, 85
believe 2, 56
belong 111
belongs   87
benchmark   197
benefit 3, 20-21, 42, 67-68, 78, 90, 144

benefits 23, 85, 96, 100-101, 109, 118-119, 127, 133, 146, 150, 246
better 10, 32, 59, 97, 110, 113, 170, 183, 191, 217, 235-236, 241
between 33, 44, 60, 62, 87-88, 97, 106, 112, 114, 121, 130-132, 150, 157, 160, 179, 231, 252, 254, 264, 266
beyond 246
bidder 267
bidders 266
biggest 139
billed 267
blockchain 79, 94
bottleneck 61, 91, 169
boundaries 38, 71
boundary 33
bounded 30, 32
bounds 38
breach 51
Breakdown 5-6, 71, 162-163, 178, 182
breaks 60
briefed 34
Briefly 181
brings 34
brought 134, 254
budget 2, 45, 71, 101, 106, 117, 139, 146, 148, 169, 184, 186, 188, 219, 242, 255, 260, 263, 272
Budgeted 201
budgeting 52, 80
budgets 164-166, 201, 254-255, 265
buffer 103
building 178, 256-257
buildout 44
burn-in 262
business 2, 10, 12, 20-22, 24, 26, 31-32, 37, 43, 46, 49, 51-55, 57-60, 62, 66, 69, 72-74, 77, 85-88, 90, 93, 95, 99-101, 103-104, 108, 111, 114, 117-118, 122-123, 126, 128-129, 131-133, 136, 154, 160, 187, 209, 220, 223, 233, 254-255, 258-259, 263
businesses 116
busywork 139
buy-in 262
calculate 198
called 127, 264
caller 69, 73-74
calling 32

cancel 57
candidates   266-267
cannot 56, 117, 186
capability   42, 161, 193
capable   10, 36, 39
capacity   26, 146
capitalize   252
capture   83, 107, 268
captured   188, 206
capturing   235
career 156, 204
carried 217
carrying   232
caseload   243
catalog   44
catching   1
category   188
caused   3, 254
causes 49, 80, 166
causing   255
celebrate   18
center 52, 100, 148
central 80, 115, 236
centrally   89, 106
centric 52
certain 65, 110, 208
Certified   168
challenge   10, 97, 236
challenged   272
challenges   101, 105, 134
champion   39
change   7-8, 18, 26, 37, 47, 54, 58, 73, 81, 88, 142-143, 152-153, 159, 162, 171, 186, 188, 190, 194, 209, 216, 225-226, 231-234, 248, 250, 254, 258, 268-269
changed   37, 189, 192, 212
changes   26, 57, 66, 71, 83, 95, 141, 148-149, 151-152, 154, 158-159, 164-165, 178, 188, 194, 231-234, 241, 255, 268, 271, 273
changing   32, 52, 118, 209
channel   40, 55, 59, 92, 107, 109, 130
channels   100, 117, 226
chargeable   201
charges   267
Charter   4, 35, 39, 141-142, 167, 220

charters 33
charting 206
charts 43, 46
checked 77, 79, 81, 100, 154-155
checklists 11, 187, 205
choices 110
choose 13, 55, 58, 89, 111-112, 131, 259
choosing 213
chosen 139, 142, 146-147, 264, 267
circuits 125
circumvent 27
claimed 3
clearly 13, 18, 29, 41, 49, 65, 76, 85, 125, 187, 203-204, 219-220, 223
client 50, 61, 82, 130, 148, 259, 262, 264
clients 59, 112, 259
clipping 133
closed 78, 187, 219, 234, 269
closely 12
Close-Out 9, 222, 268, 270
Closing 9, 264
Coaches 30
coarse 96
coherent 205
colleagues 183
collect 192, 199-200, 241
collected 32, 36, 42-43, 57, 70, 107
collection 42-43, 45, 47, 200
combine 65, 67, 103
combined 103
coming 222
command 74
comments 222, 262
commercial 213
commit 151, 187, 214
commitment 199, 213, 254
committed 32, 206
committee 161, 196, 231
common 79, 104-105, 123, 185, 189, 221
community 152, 184, 192
companies 3, 87, 91, 236
company 1-2, 10
compare 256, 272

compared   166, 195
comparing   164
comparison   13, 254
compass   36
compatible   233, 252
compelling   31, 73
competitor   2, 254
complete   3, 11, 13, 34, 53, 56, 63, 136, 167, 175, 179, 181, 183, 204, 206, 212, 214, 263, 267-268
completed   14, 33-34, 37-38, 141, 164, 170, 175, 181, 187, 240, 269
completely   1, 216
completing   162
completion   32, 35, 136, 165-166, 176, 237, 252, 256
complex   10, 54, 128, 148, 225, 257
complexity   82, 151
compliance   1, 160, 238, 272
complied   240
comply   267
component   23, 42, 76, 88, 132, 134-135
components   43, 46, 53, 86, 106, 117, 160, 224, 227
compress   99
compute   14
computer   161
computers   22
computing   54, 91
concept   159, 200
concerned   20
concerns   2, 23, 91, 96, 208, 261
concise   152
concrete   244
condition   83
conditions   79, 193, 241, 266
conduct   116, 195
conducted   70, 168, 205, 219, 232, 234, 246-247, 250, 267, 273
confident   175
confirm   13, 182
conflict27
conflicts   186, 240
conform   104
confronted   209
connect   108, 123, 130
connected   185

Connector	120, 132
consensus	97, 270
consider	27, 130, 172
considered	19, 57, 93, 110, 123, 131, 266-267
consist	112, 201
consistent	82, 165, 209, 252
constantly	1, 207
Constraint	5, 112, 160
consult	1
consultant	1-2, 10
consulted	202, 208
consulting	2
consume	114
consumer	86, 88, 92, 105, 110, 134
consumers	55
contact	10, 206
contacts	90
contain	21, 78, 149, 266
contained	3, 127
contains	11
content	36, 42, 64, 97, 99, 128-129, 132, 236
contents	3-4, 11
context	30, 32, 62, 181
continual	78, 80
Continuity	72, 173
contract	9, 98, 168, 175, 180, 201, 230, 240, 266-269
Contractor	8, 159, 164, 260, 266
contracts	165, 187, 261, 269
contribute	100, 238, 270
control	4, 71, 76, 78-83, 149, 152-153, 159, 188, 191, 227, 231, 235, 258
controlled	248, 271
controls	21, 176, 218, 259
converge	252
conversion	160
convert	54
convey	3
cooperate	191
coordinate	55, 219
Copyright	3
corporate	2
correct	41, 76, 126, 135, 185
corrective	80, 150, 164-165, 187

correctly 58
correspond 11-12
counsel 222
counting 169
coupled 45
coupling 106, 114
course 37, 257
covering 11
crashes 58, 92
create 19, 42, 54, 94, 158, 197, 206
created 139, 143, 146, 149, 167, 182, 187, 217
creating 10
creation 215
creativity 73
credible 167, 191
crisis 22
criteria 4, 7, 11-12, 38, 73, 138, 149, 153, 156, 158, 192, 194-195, 221, 226, 268
CRITERION 4, 18, 29, 41, 49, 65, 76, 85
critical 31-32, 36, 43, 72, 79-80, 95, 160, 167, 169, 174, 180, 187, 228, 235, 244
criticized 245
crucial 228
crystal 13
Cultural 65, 145
culture 197, 203, 223, 225, 242
current 35, 41, 44, 47, 61, 80, 89-90, 106-108, 110, 112, 114, 116, 123, 126, 131-132, 135, 154, 161, 165, 167, 175, 195, 200, 203, 223, 227, 243, 259
currently 34, 78, 82, 94, 118, 128, 136, 164, 235, 246
custom 60, 66, 120, 125, 129
customer 25, 31-32, 36-37, 39, 47, 51, 57, 74, 77-78, 90, 97, 107, 125, 154-155, 159, 209, 214, 216, 231, 241, 263
customers 3, 20, 24, 32, 34, 38, 46, 49, 70, 112, 130, 134, 155, 160, 173, 210, 214, 230, 267
customize 66
customized 2, 106
cut-down 257
cutting 214
damage 3
Dashboard 11, 79
dashboards 83
database 52, 58-59

databases   50, 54, 58, 60
day-to-day   80, 174
deadline   267
deadlines   173
decide 71, 195
decision   8, 204, 222, 227, 235-236
decisions   59, 66-67, 70, 142, 205, 227, 235-236, 240-241, 245, 259, 266, 271
decompress   128
decouple   80, 88
dedicated   10, 130
deeper   13
defect 41
defective   215
defects   41, 237
define 4, 29, 31, 155, 163, 236
defined   13, 18, 21, 29, 34, 41, 49, 65, 76, 85, 146, 159, 162, 187, 197, 203, 219, 228, 237, 251
defines 178, 190
defining   10, 160, 223
definite   78
definition   160, 188, 214, 220
degree   244-247, 252-253
-degree   2
delays 183, 210
delegated   39
delete 189
deletions   83
deliver 20, 31, 117-118, 132, 137, 191, 243
delivered   120, 153, 167, 178, 193, 241, 271
delivering   62, 212, 246
delivery   131, 147, 175, 215, 225, 268
demand   90, 214, 267
demands   47, 252-253
department   10, 62, 229, 266
depend   229
dependence 111
dependency 272
dependent   141, 153
deploy 23, 131
deployed   82, 93, 122
deployment   237
derive 173

describe 70, 142, 156, 181, 260
described 3, 201, 233
describes 180
describing 38
deserve 270
deserving 230
design 12, 66, 70, 91, 93-94, 106, 130, 136, 147, 161, 273
designed 10, 12, 57, 70, 74, 111
designing 10, 101, 135
desirable 133
desired 23, 33, 63, 71, 102, 178, 234, 257
detail 142, 162
detailed 139, 146, 151-152, 169
detailing 259
detect 79, 117
determine 12, 49, 86, 146, 187, 192, 270
determined 95, 167, 199-200
determines 134, 189
develop 26, 61, 65, 68, 149, 162-163, 211, 244
developed 12, 33-35, 66, 71, 73, 152, 160-161, 180, 194, 199, 233, 256-257
developer 209
developers 66-67, 69, 214
developing 246
device 237, 239
devices 24, 97, 108-109, 237
diagnostic 217
diagram 6, 175-176, 186
diagrams 206
dictates 185
Dictionary 5, 52, 164
differ 54-55, 59, 118, 128, 135
difference 87, 112, 130, 132, 146, 179, 189, 235
different 10, 24, 30, 32, 35, 39, 50-51, 56-57, 92, 106, 110, 114, 136, 213, 236, 270
difficult 49, 136-137, 169, 171, 174, 178, 194
digital 45, 67, 94, 101
direct 59, 190, 201
direction 37
directly 3, 32, 42, 46, 144, 271
Directory 8, 240
disabled 133
Disagree 13, 18, 29, 41, 49, 65, 76, 85

disaster 185
discard62, 106
discovered 71
discrete 201
dishonest 113
disparate 92
dispersed 107
display 43, 173
displayed 32, 44-46, 170, 183
disposal 239
disputes 245, 268
dissimilar 114
distribute 240
disturbing 109
Divided 27, 39-40, 48, 64, 75, 84, 137
document 12, 33, 69, 73-74, 142, 149, 152, 154, 160, 219, 235, 241
documented 34, 76, 80, 82-83, 103, 140, 146, 158-160, 167-168, 188, 195, 203, 228, 238, 251, 262
documents 10, 181, 188, 266
dollar 255
domain 102
dominating 242
driving 90
dropped 168
duplicate 124
duplicates 118
Duration 6, 158, 162, 165, 167, 180, 183
durations 30, 185
during 37, 50, 53, 60, 68, 139, 171, 177, 188-189, 202, 205, 209, 215-216, 218, 222, 236-237, 255, 259, 267, 270, 273
dynamic 91, 123
dynamics 35
eagerly 2
earlier 92
earned 8, 201, 256-257
easily 66, 158, 244
economic 135, 267
economies 144
economy 227
eDiscovery 74, 235
edition 11
editorial 3

educated 1
education 80
effect 167, 264
effective 20, 43-44, 107, 165, 184, 217, 235, 237-239, 246, 259, 273
effects 144-145, 207
efficient 36, 61, 91, 229, 273
effort 72, 149, 224-225, 238, 250
efforts 37, 104, 117, 187, 196, 238, 273
either 172
electronic 3
element 255
elements 12, 61-62, 86, 122, 142, 159, 165, 167, 200, 202, 205, 220, 228, 241, 255
elicit 107, 199
Eliminate 42, 186
eliminated 196
embarking 31
embrace 225
emerging 1, 55, 77, 246
employed 114
employee 195, 260
employees 23-24, 102, 114, 123, 196, 237
employer 31
employers 143
empower 10
empowered 238
enable 57, 134, 273
enabled 96
enabling 94
enacted 52, 55-56
encourage 74
encouraged 202, 238
endpoint 102, 108, 119
endpoints 108
end-users 215
energy 1
engage 242, 244, 253
engagement 33, 143, 207, 220, 243, 248
engineer 50, 58
engineered 71
enhance 253
enhancing 93

enjoys 206
enough   10, 26, 110, 155-156, 209, 246, 264
enrichment   63
ensure 30, 39, 51, 71, 95, 102, 127, 153, 160, 165, 195, 200, 203, 240, 242, 245, 267, 272
ensured   98
ensuring   12, 256-257
entails 237
entered   57
Enterprise   3-16, 18-28, 30-40, 44, 46, 48, 50-55, 57, 60, 64, 67, 69, 71-72, 74-75, 77-79, 83-84, 88-91, 93-109, 111, 113, 115-119, 123-125, 127, 129, 131-133, 136-141, 143-154, 156-165, 167-171, 173-197, 199, 201-203, 205-207, 209-217, 219-225, 227-231, 233-235, 237, 240, 242, 244, 246, 248, 250-252, 254-260, 262-266, 268-273
entire 55, 133, 214
entities 149
entity 3
envisaged   147
equipment   224, 243
equipped   38
equitably   39, 245
equivalent   50, 187
errors 19, 114, 246
escalated   265
escalation   194, 273
essential   245
establish   65, 191, 209
estimate   100, 148, 184, 188-190, 221, 263
estimated   32, 35, 191, 211, 260, 272
estimates   6, 34, 148, 165-166, 180, 187-189, 194, 219, 223, 255
Estimating   6, 183, 188, 191-192
estimator   189-190
evaluate   67, 73, 159, 164
evaluated   70
evaluating   56, 73
evaluation   149, 165, 221, 250, 253
events 181, 258-259, 267
Everyday   1
everyone   37, 39, 199
everything   235
evidence   13, 198, 212, 230, 258, 266

evolution 41
evolve 129, 131, 136
evolving 108
exactly 47, 69, 95, 117, 203
Example 4, 11, 15, 160, 164
examples 10-11
exceed 162, 186
excellence 10
exception 134
excess 255
excessive 258
exchange 59, 90, 110, 128, 252
excited 1
excluding 45
execute 60, 64, 264
executed 43, 45, 57, 233
executes 53
Executing 7, 215, 227
execution 59, 64, 103, 124, 126, 149, 160, 240, 267, 272
executive 10, 67
existence 213
existing 12, 44, 52, 58, 60, 63, 69, 74, 89, 102, 118-119, 122, 128, 130, 142, 158, 254
exists 93, 113, 128, 175
expect 95-96, 118, 149
expected 23, 30, 52, 94, 140, 147, 228, 235, 238
expense 254-255
expenses 242
experience 59, 107, 115, 131, 148, 183, 189, 203, 237, 259-260, 270
expert 266
expertise 148-149, 187, 189
experts 39, 187
expiration 175
explained 12
explore 244
export 145
exposed 133
expressed 149
extend 58, 66, 92
extensible 111
extensive 2
extent 13, 19-21, 30, 147, 238, 259

external   1-2, 37, 102, 104, 122, 207, 255, 266
facilitate   13, 52, 83, 122, 133, 221, 252
facilities   52, 102, 154, 238
facing 27, 211
fact-based   244
factor 221
factors 26, 95, 129, 136, 141, 161, 176, 191, 215, 250
failed   103, 125
failover 23
failure 25, 264
failures 110
fairly   39
falling   168
familiar 11
fashion 3, 36
Favorable   254
feasible   191, 211
feature 12
features   263
feedback   36-37, 107, 204
feeling 1
fields   251
figure   42
finalize 222
finalized   15
finally   118, 152
financial   32, 93, 95, 99, 108, 115, 146-147, 164
fingertips   12
finish   167, 171, 173, 176, 184, 256-257
finished   136, 173
flexible 27, 32, 94
focused   27
follow 82, 175, 262, 264
followed   35, 83, 112, 150, 164, 187, 224
following   11, 13
follow-on   265
follow-up   147, 189
forecast   256
forecasts   167
foreseen   139
forget 12
forgotten   216
formal 9, 152, 161, 232, 252, 262

formally   151, 187
format 12, 51, 54, 57, 62, 104
formats   50-51, 56-57
formatted   58
formed 30, 32
forming   224
formula   14
Formulate   29
forward   2
forwarded   121
foster   203
framework   88, 112, 132, 147, 200
frequency   81, 197, 200
frequent   223
frequently   144, 244, 246
friends 2
fulfill   38
full-scale   66
fulltime 206
function   129, 231, 267
functional   111, 164-165, 243
functions   50, 88, 104, 125, 154-155, 203, 241
funding   132, 153, 251
further 11, 24
future   10, 21, 42, 57, 71, 80-81, 87, 115, 165
gained 2, 77
gateway   131
gather 13, 40-41
gathering   33, 154, 214
general   38, 172, 182, 223, 263
generally   229
generate   67
generated   43, 51, 65, 124, 165, 195
generation   11, 67
generic   2
getting 2, 58, 86, 208
govern 252
governance   95, 100, 106
governed   106
gracefully   91
grained   96
granted   193
graphics   24

292

graphs 11, 46
ground 46
grouped 171
groups 202, 230, 252
growing 117, 124
growth 81, 90
guarantee 111
guaranteed 40
Guidance 197
guidelines 149, 267
guides 149
guiding 237-238
gyroscope 36
handle 91, 96, 99, 120, 125, 177, 241
handled 118, 135, 221-222
handling 51, 111, 134
happen 21, 212
happened 90
happening 22, 217
happens 10, 56, 58-60, 64, 119, 154, 191, 211, 218, 247, 268
hardly 256
hardware 109, 161
having 92
hazards 217-218
hazmat 259
health 150
healthy 195
helpful 46, 87, 202
helping 10, 147, 251
hidden 123
highest 24
high-level 33, 37, 154
highlight 2
hinder 203
hindrance 237
hiring 83
historical 192
history 169, 181
hitting 256
holiday 2
Honestly 2
hosted 44
hosting 86

humans   10
hybrid 90, 119
hypotheses   49
hypothesis   272
identified   3, 27, 31, 34, 39, 41, 43-44, 54, 56, 139, 150-151, 166-168, 172, 188, 198, 202-203, 205, 211, 213, 216, 218-220, 241, 254, 270
identify 1, 12-13, 58, 141, 144, 158, 164-165, 174, 181, 192, 202, 206, 215, 237, 254-255
identity 88, 113, 115
imbedded   77
immediate   46, 53
impact 7, 34, 38, 41-42, 44-45, 47, 75, 139, 158, 193, 211, 213, 215, 228, 233-234, 250, 259, 273
impacted   42, 46, 158
impacts   183, 224
implement   24, 76, 92, 126, 129, 137, 201
import 145
importance   253
important   25, 27, 50, 52, 63, 67, 97, 100, 115-116, 120, 123, 127, 131, 133, 146, 158, 193, 207, 245, 248, 250, 264
importing   104
improper   237
improve   4, 12, 63, 65, 68, 141, 178, 241, 246, 258, 265
improved   2, 53, 66, 70, 82
improves   140
improving   230
inactive   117, 189
inadequate   1
incentives   83
incident   235-236
include   94, 99, 121, 153, 220, 224
included   4, 10, 27, 29, 104, 154, 191, 215, 260, 266, 269
includes   12, 47
including   30, 37, 39, 59, 71, 141, 160, 255
incoming   111
in-coming   196
increase   19, 46, 52, 96, 112
increased   47, 62
incumbent   35
incurrence   255
in-depth   11, 13
indicate   44, 83, 238

indicated   80
indicators   165, 196, 213
indirect   165, 190, 254-255
indirectly   3
individual   67, 184, 203, 242, 252, 261, 270
industrial   30
industry   1-2, 32, 205
influence   143, 147, 204, 208, 235-236, 270
influenced   266
influences   207
inform 50, 246
informal   252
informed   135, 139
ingrained   81
inherent   203
inhibit 65
in-house   2, 195, 266-267
initial   104, 117, 168
initially 153
initiate 165
initiated   191, 233
Initiating   4, 73, 139
Initiation   273
initiative   13, 144
Innovate   65
innovative   191, 227
inputs 30, 38, 77, 151
inside 22
insight 122
insights 1-2, 11
inspect 107
instance   56, 63
Instead 2
instructed   153
insurance   259
integrate   24-25, 53, 68-70, 72, 74, 85, 87, 89, 94-95, 101-102, 107-109, 111, 113, 121-122, 125, 128, 131-132, 149
integrated   21, 46, 52, 56, 58-60, 62, 67, 73-74, 89-90, 94, 97, 99, 101, 104-105, 108-109, 113, 121-122, 124, 128, 140
integrity   24, 33, 110, 134, 233
intend 87, 98
intended   3, 73
intense 99

INTENT 18, 29, 41, 49, 65, 76, 85
intention   3
intentions   237
intents 146
interact   59, 134
interest 117, 217, 230, 266
interested   86, 251, 267, 271
interests   25
interface   24, 70, 119, 124, 129, 198
interfaced   96
interfaces   24, 71, 102, 107, 160
internal   1, 3, 37, 59, 102, 104, 120, 125, 160, 165, 207, 258
interpret   13
interview   1
intranet   100
introduced   102, 158, 244
invest 26
investing   2
investment   20, 121, 200
invoices   224
invoke 95
invoking   129
involved   20, 22, 27, 46, 150, 153, 168, 214, 227-229, 245, 268
isolated   254
issued 197
issues   18, 21, 25-26, 71, 140, 150, 158, 177, 185, 197-198, 202, 212, 219, 223, 240, 254, 265, 273
istoppers   212
itself   3, 23
jointly 71, 253
justified 224
Knowing   150
knowledge   1-2, 12, 37, 46, 59, 77, 79, 83, 127, 131, 203, 206, 268
labeling   57, 109, 129
languages   113
larger 27
latency   119
latest   11, 51, 166
lawsuits   210
leader 39, 243
leaders 30, 37, 207, 244

leadership 34, 133, 243
learned 1, 9, 80, 83, 199, 262, 264, 270, 272
learning 79, 235, 237
ledger 182
legacy 30, 78, 114, 119
length 111
lesson 264, 270-271
lessons 9, 66, 83, 199, 262, 270, 272
letters 32
Leveling 172
levels 24, 81, 100, 111, 144, 166, 195, 199, 202, 214, 218
leverage 36, 83, 192, 226, 243
leveraged 37
leveraging 246
liability 3
license 131
licensed 3
licensing 44
Lifetime 12, 119
likelihood 212, 217
likely 56, 137, 193, 222, 236
limited 12
linked 32, 60, 92, 235
linking 259
listed 200
Litigation 210
little 2
loaded 22
locally 106
location 236
logical 85, 94, 176-177
logistics 47
longer 1
long-term 81
looked 1
looking 99
loosely 45
losses 23
lowest 165, 175
machine 51
magazine 266
mainstream 129
maintain 47, 76-77, 80, 195

maintained 180, 202, 239, 252, 267
makers 227
making 59, 96, 199, 204, 251
manage 49, 67, 89, 98, 124, 140, 142, 149, 153, 156, 161, 171, 174, 186, 189, 207, 212, 215, 241, 248, 258
manageable 30, 133
managed 10, 18, 106, 132, 136, 153, 262
management 5-7, 11-12, 19-20, 25, 30, 39, 50, 53, 62, 64, 68, 70-71, 74, 87, 93, 97, 106-108, 115-116, 127, 129, 132-133, 137, 139, 146, 148-150, 152, 159, 167, 181, 183, 186-188, 193, 195, 199, 201-202, 204-205, 207, 209, 211, 213, 216, 219-220, 223, 225, 227-230, 238, 241, 250-251, 254, 256, 258-259, 262, 268
manager 10, 12, 18, 32, 39, 150-151, 168, 213, 216, 222, 229
managers 4, 27, 138, 149, 165, 180-181, 202, 213
manages 116, 141, 261
managing 4, 50, 78, 91, 97, 99, 103, 138, 143-144, 223, 238
Mandated 215
mandatory 233, 271
manner 23, 44, 99, 165, 205, 227, 253-255
manual 196
mapped 31
mapping 228
margin 254
market 113-114, 134, 141, 209, 221, 227, 257
marketable 209
marketer 10
Marketing 96, 144
markets 129, 131, 136
mashups 118
master 50, 52, 185
material 196, 201, 254, 259
materials 3, 226, 242
matrices 157
Matrix 4-7, 144, 156, 201, 215
matter 39, 118, 244
maximize 246
maximum 63
meaning 171
meaningful 209
measurable 38, 140, 237, 246
measure 4, 12, 22, 34, 36, 41-42, 45, 53, 65, 147, 192-193, 198, 252
measured 43, 77, 253

measures   43-44, 83, 195-196, 217, 227-228, 232
mechanical   3
mechanics   232
mechanism   96, 232
mechanisms   93, 128, 147, 158
medium   244, 257
meeting   31, 77, 101, 203, 207, 230, 236, 240, 242-243
meetings   35-36, 38, 40, 152, 202, 209, 227, 243, 267, 273
member   8, 34, 179, 229, 242, 246-247
members   1, 30, 33, 36, 38-40, 146, 168, 180, 185, 202-203, 206, 208, 215, 240, 242-246, 253
membership   245-246, 266
memory   52
mentors   258
message   50, 53-55, 57-58, 60-61, 65, 67, 74, 79-80, 85-87, 91-92, 95, 97-99, 101, 103, 105, 108-110, 114, 117, 120-130, 134-135
messages   45, 50, 56-58, 61, 65, 67, 80, 82, 86, 88, 91, 98, 103, 105-107, 109-111, 114-115, 122-124, 126-127, 132, 134-135, 249, 271
messaging   22, 50-51, 57, 60-61, 64, 82, 91-92, 94-96, 98, 117, 120
metadata   51
method   94, 225, 245
methods   37, 45, 108, 160, 192, 195, 205, 215, 220
metrics 6, 42, 83, 197-198, 209, 258
Microsoft   181
middleware   89, 98, 110, 117-118, 129, 136
migration   42, 47, 78, 92
milestone   5, 173, 175, 205
milestones   39, 143, 165, 167, 171, 175
minimal   53
minimise   226
minimize   51, 114, 139, 165
minimum   56, 239, 260
minority   25
minutes   31, 240, 266
missing 101, 171, 273
mission 118, 217, 238
mitigate   144, 212
mitigated   2, 270
mitigating   150
mitigation   167

mixture 109
mix-ups   237
mobile 24, 30, 38, 53, 97, 100, 109, 118
Modeling   51, 200
models 72, 88, 101, 119, 132
modern   181
modified   70, 106, 115
modify 112
Monday   1
monetary   20, 100
monitor   73, 80-82, 192, 219
monitored   139, 169, 180, 184
monitoring   8, 76, 78-81, 164, 177, 206, 213, 250
monthly   135, 165
months 1
morning   1
motion 121
motivate   252
motivated   102
motivation   144
motive 199
moving   47
multimedia   30, 53
multiple   50, 54-55, 61, 85, 87, 102-103, 110, 113, 124, 127, 258
nearest   14
necessary   56, 72, 146, 161, 165, 192, 233, 245, 250
needed   2, 19, 22, 26-27, 30, 80-81, 142, 154, 183, 189, 199, 202, 206, 220, 222-223, 225, 227, 248, 270
negative   42, 186, 226
negatively   228
negotiate   267
neither 3
network   6, 32, 62, 68, 91, 123, 175-176, 186
Neutral 13, 18, 29, 41, 49, 65, 76, 85
normal 81
notice 3, 146
notified   268
number   27, 33, 40, 48, 64, 75, 84, 86, 108, 137, 214, 274
numbers   243
numerous   268
object 103, 129
objection   20, 25

objective 10, 141, 158, 165, 189, 235
objectives 2, 20, 24-25, 29, 32, 95, 140, 149, 151, 206, 212, 217, 220, 230, 238, 241, 246, 259, 273
objects 102
obligates 180
observe 204
observed 72
observing 160
obstacles 27, 173, 191
obtain 262
obtained 36, 161
obvious 245
obviously 13
occurred 95, 211
occurring 68, 139, 211
occurs 22, 60, 215, 251, 264
offered 82, 87, 116
offering 115
offerings 119
office 222, 229, 268
Officer 1
officers 222
officials 269
one-time 10
ongoing 42, 77, 169, 184, 238
on-going 219
online 127
on-site 241
operate 113
operating 8, 82, 108-109, 126, 136, 164, 242
operation 29, 77, 136, 184, 193
operations 12, 26, 51, 71, 81, 83, 98, 102, 119, 193
operators 82, 197, 267
opponent 236
opposed 249
optimal 68-69, 93, 260
optimize 22
option 259
options 18, 117
oracle 122, 132
ordered 1
ordering 127, 266
orders 266-267

organize	31, 125, 148, 182
organized	55, 113, 172, 180, 267
orient	77
oriented	53, 57, 91, 98, 102-103, 117, 126, 130, 205
original	165, 168, 185, 235, 238
originator	58
others	137, 181, 185, 191, 194, 208-209, 232, 236, 238, 270
otherwise	3, 65
ourselves	73
outages	19
outcome	13, 144, 178, 266
outcomes	63, 68, 72, 191, 237, 257-258
outlier	172
output	36, 43, 79, 83
outputs	38, 77, 177, 224
outside	74, 141, 187, 227
Outsource	268
overall	12-13, 20, 68, 160, 176, 223, 235, 242, 250, 260, 264, 273
overcome	191
overhead	32, 164-165, 201-202
overheads	220
overlook	208
overlooked	140, 227
overruns	164, 255
oversees	140
oversight	159, 196
overtime	171
owners	162
ownership	43, 77
package	124, 165
packaged	110
packages	135, 165, 201
packaging	132, 259
packets	57
Padding	189
painlessly	117
parallel	176
parameters	79
Pareto	206
particular	33, 46, 86
parties	2, 150, 267-268
partner	96, 116, 125
partners	20, 77, 102, 122, 125, 146, 245

pattern 69, 87, 92, 101, 172
Patterns 3-9, 11-16, 18-28, 30-40, 48, 64, 69, 75, 77-79, 84, 86, 93-94, 101, 103, 106, 117, 130-131, 135-141, 143-154, 156-165, 167-171, 173-197, 199, 201-203, 205-207, 209-217, 219-225, 227-231, 233-235, 237, 240, 242, 244, 246, 248, 250-252, 254-260, 262-266, 268-273
paying 70
payment 224, 268
pending 234
people 10, 42, 59, 67, 85, 110, 123, 131, 133, 144, 202, 206, 209-210, 212, 214, 217, 230, 242, 257-258, 264
perceived 133
percent 121
percentage 93, 157, 197
perform 35-36, 39, 54, 69, 73, 149, 170, 217, 262
performed 52, 156, 169-170, 202, 211, 221, 240
performing 66, 139, 201
perhaps 257
period 164, 189, 201, 212, 246
periods 164
permission 3
person 3, 173, 190
personal 33, 64
personally 156
personnel 20, 83, 91, 108, 151, 186-187, 238
phases 118, 171, 188, 209, 271
phones 97
pieces 98
pitfalls 25
placed 114, 221
placements 237
planned 43, 45, 80, 83, 139, 164, 168, 183, 211-212
planning 5, 11, 83, 141, 146, 149, 151-152, 175, 177, 230, 238, 264, 273
platform 57, 62, 89, 100, 103, 124, 126-127, 130-131, 136
platforms 46, 72, 94, 109, 247
played 102
playing 2
pocket 184
pockets 184
points 27, 40, 47-48, 64, 67, 75, 84, 91, 113, 137, 200
policies 149, 259
policy 51, 68, 127, 147, 160, 177, 266

Political	65, 145
portable	114
portals	118
portfolio	87, 98, 251
portion	2, 58
position	151, 203
positioned	107, 191
positions	31, 237
positive	161
possess	245
possible	55, 57, 65, 67, 76, 97, 245
potential	19, 68, 73, 164, 211, 217, 255
practical	65, 76, 121, 230
practice	90, 151, 187, 267
practiced	140
practices	12, 26, 83, 129, 131, 136, 203, 246, 258, 263
precaution	3
predictive	26
preferred	225
pre-filled	11
premise	74, 89
premises	122
prepare	67, 86, 187, 204, 243, 248, 273
prepared	1, 188
preparing	185, 215, 270
present	42, 47, 81, 105, 136, 152, 167, 220, 225, 244
presented	1, 125
presenting	238
preserve	35
pressures	173
prevent	212, 219, 242, 246
prevented	22, 237
preventing	24
preventive	217
previous	37, 173, 186, 260, 265
previously	148, 233
primary	60, 78, 92, 112, 178, 255
principle	225
Principles	67, 149
priorities	43-44, 107
prioritize	47
Priority	45, 172
privacy	56

Private 267
probably 179, 215
problem 18, 22, 29-30, 37-39, 43, 45, 60, 215, 230, 235, 244, 256
problems 20-22, 25, 27, 68, 80, 154, 198-200, 210, 250
procedure 95, 127, 164, 237, 267
procedures 12, 80, 82-83, 103, 161, 164, 167, 177, 188, 196, 200, 235
proceed 213
proceeding 183, 185
process 4-10, 12, 26, 30, 33-38, 41-46, 49-64, 66, 70, 72-73, 77-83, 90, 92, 122, 139-140, 146, 153-154, 156, 159-161, 165, 177, 181, 187, 193, 199-200, 203, 209, 214, 219, 222, 224, 227, 235, 240-241, 245, 250, 256-259, 261, 264-267
processed 56, 59, 82, 266
processes 1, 31, 46, 49-55, 58-60, 62, 83, 121, 137, 139-140, 146-147, 159-160, 187, 200-201, 223, 228, 233, 251, 263-264, 272
processing 50, 53-55, 57-58, 60, 62
processors 54
procuring 227
produce 1, 147, 177, 224, 230
produced 146, 272
producing 157
product 3, 33, 96, 105, 112, 123, 132, 134, 142, 152, 158, 160, 186, 193, 209, 215, 229-230, 233, 241, 256-258, 262, 264, 271-273
production 47, 57, 124, 144
productive 21
products 3, 61, 70, 124-125, 129, 131-132, 136, 141, 146-147, 153, 157, 213, 230, 234, 244, 250, 272
profession 209
profile 238
profits 193
program 22, 140-141, 147, 149, 209, 212, 227, 250-251
programme 146
programs 104, 149, 230, 238
progress 34, 147, 192, 196, 199, 227, 237, 250-252
prohibited 164
prohibits 267

project 4-6, 8-11, 18, 22, 25-27, 34, 42, 45-46, 53-54, 67, 72-73, 79, 83, 93, 97, 101, 103-104, 106-107, 110, 116, 118, 120-121, 124, 127, 130, 136, 138-141, 143-153, 156, 158-163, 165, 167-171, 173-176, 178-188, 190-196, 202-203, 205-207, 210-216, 219-220, 222-225, 227-231, 233-234, 240, 250-252, 255-257, 259-260, 262-265, 269-273
projected 42, 202
projects 4, 25, 42, 44, 71, 80, 85-86, 90, 97, 103, 107-108, 138, 140-141, 144, 146-147, 149, 157, 161, 163, 180-181, 186, 189, 194, 205, 213, 216, 229-230, 256-258, 270
promise 118
promptly 265
proofing 72
propagate 62
Proper 267
properly 37, 139, 232, 238, 266
proportion 105
proposal 173, 221
proposals 181, 221
proposed 68, 74, 148, 260-261
protect 110, 266
protected 243
protocols 39, 134
proved 263
provide 22, 72, 103, 119, 121, 126, 143, 147, 152, 155, 164, 175, 191, 201-202, 244, 253, 258
provided 2, 14, 46, 76, 111, 113, 195, 243, 273
provider 88, 103, 120
providers 72
provides 173
providing 142-143
provision 150, 236
provisions 266
Public 220, 266-267
published 221
publisher 3
purchase 10, 219, 222, 267
purchased 97
purchasing 1-2
purpose 4, 12, 51, 136, 140-141, 144, 178-179, 192, 199, 223, 236, 244, 250
purposes 141
pursuing 2

putting 124
qualified   39, 149, 219
quality 6, 8, 12, 46, 83, 87, 100, 146-147, 158, 180-181, 187, 189, 193, 195, 197, 199-200, 203, 205-206, 220, 223, 231, 235, 237, 241, 258, 272
quarters   255
question   13, 18, 29, 41, 49, 65, 76, 85, 146, 199
questions   10-11, 13, 183, 207
queues 114, 130
quickly 12, 53, 58-59, 63, 190, 210
radical 86
raising 147
rather 270
rating 222, 246-247
rational   165, 201
rationale   220, 223, 236
reached   114, 266
readiness   219, 226
readings   81, 147
realistic   148, 165, 215, 247
realize 2
realized   53, 263
realizing   1, 114
really   10, 62, 95, 118, 202
reason 50
reasonable   132, 168, 219, 223
reasonably   165
reasons   31, 92, 151, 165
reassess   150
receipt 237
receive   11-12, 32, 69, 73, 86-87, 92, 105, 109-110, 122, 222, 249
received   34, 65, 222, 224, 272
receiver   55, 63, 69, 73, 85, 91, 95, 99, 124, 129
receivers   225
receives   87, 95, 130, 247
receiving   86, 88, 91, 132, 135
recent 213
recipient   21, 268
recognize   4, 18-22, 25-27
recognized   19, 21, 23, 25-26, 205, 244
recognizes   18
recommend   137, 159

record 195, 200
recorded 219
recording 3
records 180, 195, 201-202, 239, 267, 269
recovered 119
Recovery 134, 211
recruit 196
recurrence 217
reduce 72, 144, 212, 258
reduced 217
reducing 42, 77
redundancy 91
reference 94, 118, 266
references 274
referring 104
reflect 167, 270
refresh 64
refreshed 2, 64
regarding 160, 230
region 144
Register 4, 7, 143, 211, 215, 223, 249, 259
registry 99, 129
regular 26, 34, 38, 59, 260
regularly 33, 35, 40, 158, 181, 227
regulatory 240, 272
reject 153, 159, 225
relate 93, 106, 127, 233
related 18, 54, 67, 79, 102, 126, 135, 140, 158, 193, 195, 203, 232, 256, 271
relating 37, 193
relation 145, 237
relative 150, 196, 253
relatively 86
release 188, 271
released 231
releases 260
relevant 38, 113, 158, 161, 193, 203, 213, 240, 254, 266
reliable 38, 217, 223
reliably 120
relieved 2
remain 113
remaining 119, 185, 191
remedies 46

remote 61, 89, 99, 119, 127
remove 42, 61, 71
repeat 58
repeatable 209
rephrased 12
replace 142
replanning 165
replier 116
report 8, 81, 173, 188, 197, 229, 252, 260, 270
reported 158, 187, 201, 249, 256
reporting 59, 81, 137, 151, 153, 158, 165, 181, 197, 255
reports 2, 54, 63, 143, 149, 153, 168, 224
repository 37, 74, 188
represent 133, 233-234
reproduced 3
request 8, 59, 86-88, 104, 115, 119, 129, 152, 194, 231, 233-234
requested 3, 194, 234
requesting 267
requests 120, 125, 222, 231, 267
require 30, 33, 35-36, 39, 45, 68, 177, 215
required 29, 33, 36-37, 54, 57, 62, 131, 147, 150-151, 154, 169, 175, 183, 203, 206, 242, 251, 271, 273
requiring 143, 268
research 116, 159, 213, 270
resemble 221
reserved 3
reserves 202
reside 60, 104
resiliency 60, 97
resilient 225
resistance 225
resolution 164
resolve 59, 134, 240, 245
resolved 25, 210, 265, 273
Resource 6-7, 50, 171, 177-179, 205, 223, 227, 230, 242
resources 2, 4, 10, 33, 38, 71, 80, 93, 108, 112, 117, 119-120, 139, 142, 144, 169, 171-172, 175, 179, 186, 189, 192, 194-195, 201, 227, 243, 248, 250, 252
respect 3, 136
respond 58, 119, 124, 202
responded 14
response 22, 77-78, 80, 82-83, 85-86, 113, 222, 261

responses   124, 215
responsive   184, 192
restart 125
result   65, 73-74, 158, 191, 194, 207, 234, 268, 271
resultant   221
resulted   81
resulting   165
results 11, 18-19, 27, 30-31, 46, 65, 67, 72, 76, 147, 172, 186, 191, 195, 246, 250-251, 262
retain   50, 85, 195-196
retention   98
retrospect   22
return   121, 200
revenues   112
review   12, 137, 148, 153, 176, 185, 195, 202, 232, 267, 273
reviewed   34, 168, 197
reviewer   245
reviews 159, 168, 175, 205, 247, 273
revised 42, 81, 166, 218
revisions   221, 268
Reward   230
rewarded   23
rewards   83, 272
rights   3
roadmap   55, 71
robust 111
robustness   173
roll-out 226
routed 98
routine 77
routing 87
running   109, 113
rushing 207
safeguards   246
sample 196, 221-222
sampling   195, 206
sanity   135
satisfied   123, 131, 135, 190, 240, 262-264, 273
satisfies 256
satisfy 23
savings 34, 42
scalable   43, 99
scaled 168

scanner 36
scanning 74
scattered 54
scenarios 42
scenes 2
schedule 5-6, 35, 71, 147, 167-168, 175, 185-186, 193, 202, 211, 224, 234, 240, 260
scheduled 64, 136, 167, 201, 227
schedules 176
scheduling 125, 205, 254
scheme 78
science 90
scopes 158
Scorecard 4, 14-16
scorecards 83
Scores 16
scoring 12
screen 243
screening 198
scripts 224
second 14, 116
secret 2
secrets 1
section 14, 27-28, 40, 47-48, 64, 75, 84, 137
sector 257
secure 86, 100
securely 109
security 39, 62, 67-68, 89, 102, 110, 112, 127, 143, 160-161, 233, 270
segment 112, 221
segmented 39
segments 32, 254
select 86, 105, 121
selected 66, 69, 149, 192
selecting 228
selection 7, 221-222, 245, 247
self-help 2
seller 180
sellers 3, 181
selling 236
-selling 254
semantics 101
sender 80, 87, 101, 120

senders 225
sending 58, 121
sensitive 62
sensor 36
sentiment 51
separate 61, 98
sequence 126, 135, 170, 176
sequencing 146, 220
series 13, 58
server 33, 60, 132
servers 74, 105
service 1-4, 10, 29, 47, 52, 57, 63, 69-71, 79, 88-89, 91, 96, 98-103, 119-120, 125-127, 129-134, 158, 193, 209, 222, 229-230, 272-273
serviced 97
services 3, 22, 29, 32, 43-44, 52, 54-55, 59, 61, 64, 72, 82, 89-90, 96-99, 102, 104, 107, 113-116, 118, 120, 122, 125, 127, 132, 134-135, 227, 243, 254, 260, 262, 268
session 61, 152
sessions 82
several 23, 58, 88, 121
severity 211
shadowing 115
shared 77, 88, 99, 147, 191, 243, 254
sharing 59, 243
shopping 1
shortened 167
should 10, 20, 26, 29, 35, 37, 43, 52-53, 56-58, 63-64, 66, 68, 70, 79, 86, 89-92, 98, 105-106, 110-113, 118, 120-121, 124, 128-130, 135, 139, 143, 145-146, 149-150, 152-153, 161, 165, 169, 173, 178-179, 184, 188-189, 194, 203-204, 209, 211-213, 215, 218, 221-222, 234, 247, 250, 254, 264, 267, 270
-should 194
showing 151
signatures 177
signed 159
signers 269
signing 267
similar 34, 37, 144, 169, 172, 207, 213
simple 43, 246, 257
simply 11, 68, 134
single 23, 43, 55, 65, 67, 98, 103, 243
single-use 10
situation 2, 21, 41, 68, 186, 189, 256

situations   80
skills   27, 180, 190, 203, 206, 210, 212, 244, 253, 273
smooth 52
soccer 1
socialize   56
software   22-23, 35, 55, 61, 63, 69, 87, 90, 92, 97, 101, 103, 110, 118, 123, 132, 140, 160, 185, 210, 213, 227, 231, 260
solicit   37, 181
solution   1, 65-76, 106, 124, 224, 260
solutions   50, 52, 54, 65-68, 72-73, 87, 91, 149
solved 22
solving 244
someone   10, 122
someones   245
something   150
sought 144
soundness   115
source 7, 56, 97, 132, 160, 217, 221
sources   53, 57, 71, 215, 223
special 76
specific   11, 23, 29, 38, 104, 130, 153, 159-160, 169, 171, 173-174, 177-178, 189, 194, 203-204, 230, 233, 237, 252, 266
specified   165, 167, 255, 271
specify 244
spectrum   95
spending   2
splitter 62
sponsor   25, 142, 150, 220, 223, 263, 270
sponsored   39
sponsors   20, 227
spring   131
spurred   117
stability 45, 95, 159
stable   57, 216, 259
staffed 33
staffing 18, 83, 148
stages   151, 237
stakes   144
standard   10, 82, 140, 151, 177, 187, 255, 260
standards   12-13, 77, 79, 81, 160, 167, 188, 233
started 11, 135, 173, 175
starting 12
start-up   240

stated 195, 201, 223, 273
statement   5, 13, 158-160, 189-190, 194, 223, 266
statements 14, 27, 38-40, 48, 64, 75, 84, 137, 158, 199, 238
static 123
statistics 40, 42
status 8, 139, 145, 150, 158, 165, 167, 229, 248, 254, 256, 260
statutory 240
steering 161, 196
storage 52
stored 49, 63, 121
straight 266
strategic 83, 136, 151, 212, 220
strategies 44, 62, 114, 134, 167, 226, 235-236
strategy 20, 24, 38, 53, 63, 92, 94, 99, 108, 111, 115, 133, 205, 209, 222, 228, 235, 254, 258, 266, 271
stream 123, 126, 135
strengths 160, 242, 263
strong 180, 258
Strongly 13, 18, 29, 41, 49, 65, 76, 85, 99
structural 95
structure 5-6, 71, 93, 111, 158, 162-163, 178, 182, 226, 237
structures 252
subfactor 221
subject 11-12, 39, 110, 152
submitted 233-234
submitting 197
subscriber 109
subsequent 167
subset 59
sub-teams 245
subtotals 189
success 22-23, 34, 42, 95, 107, 110, 139, 158, 176, 195, 206, 229, 236, 245, 250, 265, 270, 272
successful 1, 27, 71, 77, 87, 93, 97, 107, 129, 141, 146, 178, 190, 193, 209, 229
successive 62
sufficient 146, 251, 273
suggest 231, 238
suggested 80, 233-234
suitable 46, 214, 240
suites 124
Sunday 1
superior 1

supplier	46, 116, 266, 272
suppliers	38, 134, 167, 267
supplies	263
Supply 173, 214
support	3, 10, 23-24, 54, 60, 72, 77-78, 88, 97, 101-102, 104, 115, 118, 125-126, 150, 155, 177, 205, 222, 235, 261
supported	19, 24, 32, 66, 79, 101, 154
supporting	51, 89, 199
supportive	113
supports	140
surface	80
SUSTAIN	4, 85
sustaining	81
switching	46
symptom	18
synergies	144
system 12, 23, 25-26, 30, 44-45, 56-57, 61, 63, 71, 80, 82, 87, 89, 92, 96, 98-101, 104-106, 108, 110, 112-120, 122-123, 125, 127, 134, 137, 154-155, 161, 164, 195, 201-202, 204, 231, 233, 235, 238, 254, 256-257, 267
systems	1, 25, 33, 35, 41, 47, 51, 56-57, 67, 69, 74, 79, 83, 101-102, 109, 111-114, 116-118, 121-122, 126, 131, 133, 135-136, 151, 161, 225, 255-256
tactical	44
tactics 235
tailored	2
taking 56, 230
talking 10
tangible	151
tangle 202
target 39, 111, 118, 225
targeted	93
targets 140, 256
tasked 77
teaming	242
technical	65, 90, 105, 148, 160, 180, 221, 232
techniques	63, 71, 181, 188
technology	1, 26, 55-56, 67, 71-72, 81, 86, 88, 95-96, 102, 113, 115, 129, 131, 136, 154-155, 180, 211, 242-243
template	186
templates	10-11
temporal	96
temporally	88

tendency 124
tender 266
tentative 124
testable 154
test-cycle 200
tested 65
testing 31, 69, 72-73, 155, 195, 214, 258
themselves 1
therefore 217
things 264
thinking 74
thorough 234
thought 47, 207
threat 22, 116
threats 1-2
through 26, 58, 120, 236-237, 258
throughout 3, 24, 175, 180-181
Thursday 1
time-bound 38
timeframe 192
timeline 121, 124, 160, 233, 250
timeliness 51
timely 23, 36, 59, 205, 213, 227, 237, 240, 254-255, 272
Timescales 173
timetable 176
Timing 207
together 46, 56, 92, 110-111, 127
tolerable 218
toolkit 1-2
toolkits 1-2
topology 53
touched 154
toward 77, 230, 250
towards 2
traceable 201
traced 224
tracked 151, 182
tracking 31, 196, 205, 213
trademark 3
trademarks 3
tradeoff 222
trade-offs 150
trading 125

trained 32, 37-38, 215
training   24, 59, 76, 80, 82-83, 105, 205, 226, 229, 238, 243, 246-247, 272-273
Transfer   14, 28, 40, 48, 57, 60, 64, 75, 77, 83-84, 137, 261
transition   152
translated   37
transmit   55, 64, 79, 101
transport   259
travel   107, 202, 243
trends   129, 131, 136, 195, 214
triggers 206
trying   10, 217
typically   104
unaware 1
uncovered   2, 154
underlying   63, 69
underruns   164, 255
understand   32, 181, 185
understood   132, 210, 214
undertaken   108, 224
underway   141
unique 2, 37, 71, 112, 189, 194, 242
Unless   10
unprepared   1
unpriced   255
unresolved   167, 177
unsure 25
unwanted   88, 106
update   1, 185
updated   11-12, 117, 165, 176, 219, 223, 232
updates   12, 19, 83, 260
upload 242
urgent 231
useful   68, 71, 83, 87, 162, 209
usefully 12
UserID   173
usually 1, 213
utilise 86
utility   183
utilizing 1, 75
validate   61, 257
validated   33-34, 37, 168, 272
Validation   251, 257

Validity 155
valuable 10, 61-62, 129
values 124, 203, 238
variables 43, 79, 235
variance 8, 164-165, 245, 254
variances 166, 187, 254
variation 18, 30, 43-46, 77
various 89, 151
vendor 67, 70, 126, 168, 175, 187, 224
vendors 49, 53, 124, 129, 131, 136, 167
verifiable 151
verified 12, 33-34, 37, 134, 224
verify 81, 110, 147, 159, 185, 256, 268
verifying 150
version 101, 115, 260, 274
versioning 96
versions 30, 35, 98, 109
versus 243
vertically 89
vested 217
viable 87
viewpoint 270
viewpoints 270
violate 160
violation 33
Virtual 243
Vision 128, 238
visits 168
visual 46
visualize 170, 183
voices 143
volatility 259
Volumes 144
waited 2
walking 2
warehouse 53-54
warrant 241
warranty 3
wasted 93, 117
weaknesses 144, 187, 221, 263
weeknights 1
weight 221
wellbeing 195

whether 10, 25, 134, 141, 238
widespread 19
widgets 193
willing 115, 209, 214
windfall 150
wishes 105
within 1-2, 23, 42, 51, 54, 56, 67, 72, 74, 104, 123, 158, 169, 184, 197, 201, 204, 229, 233, 239, 252, 263, 267
without1, 3, 14, 25, 50, 97, 116, 165, 168, 213, 233, 268
workdays 211
worked 70, 161, 205, 207, 214
workers 130
workflow 29, 59, 86, 236
workflows 46, 66, 97
working 2, 73, 102, 115, 203-204, 210, 235, 258, 272
Worksheet 6, 183, 191
worthy 121
writing 156
written 3, 237
year-end 165
youhave 152, 213
yourself 158, 227

Printed in Germany
by Amazon Distribution
GmbH, Leipzig